Multi-stories

Multi-stories
Cross-cultural Encounters

KALPANA SAHNI

Routledge
Taylor & Francis Group
LONDON NEW YORK NEW DELHI

First published 2010
by Routledge
912 Tolstoy House, 15–17 Tolstoy Marg, New Delhi 110 001

Simultaneously published in the UK
by Routledge
2 Park Square, Milton Park, Abingdon, Oxfordshire OX14 4RN

First issued in paperback 2015

Routledge is an imprint of the Taylor & Francis Group, an informa business

© 2010 Kalpana Sahni

Typeset by
Star Compugraphics Private Limited
D–156, Second Floor
Sector 7, Noida 201 301

British Library Cataloguing-in-Publication Data
A catalogue record of this book is available from the British Library

ISBN 13: 978-1-138-66265-0 (pbk)
ISBN 13: 978-0-415-58564-4 (hbk)

To my son, Martand

Contents

List of Plates

Acknowledgements

The following holders of copyright are owed thanks for their assistance and permission to reproduce visual material:

1. The Black Virgin in a Cathedral in Frauenchiemsee, Germany. Reinhard Weidl

2. The Black Virgin in the Theatine Church in Munich, Germany. Stephanie Faber

3. The J. Paul Getty Museum, Los Angeles
   Artist: Illuminator: Unknown
   Title: Josaphat Meeting a Blind Man and a Beggar
   Date: 1469
   Medium: Ink, colored washes, and tempera colors on paper
   Size: Leaf: 28.6 × 20.3 cm (11¼ × 8 in)

4. The Coronation Mantle of King Roger II of Sicily. Kunsthistorisches Museum, Vienna

5. Gentile da Fabriano. *Adoration of the Magi*. Uffizi Gallery, Florence, Ufficio Permessi — Polo Museale Florentino

6. Coin of the Roman Emperor Philip the Arab. Thibaut Marchal

7. Armenian Altar Curtain in the Church of St. James, Jerusalem. Dickran Kouymjian

8. Bayan Tuyakbaeva in Yasawi. Romi Khosla

9. Havana Marking with Raffi, the finalist of *Afghan Idol*. Havana Marking

Introduction

◉

Acamel in the old part of Jerusalem is dressed up for tourists with woven textile bands of a Kullu shawl design. Nearby, the proud possessions of the Armenian Church of St James are the block-printed cotton altar curtains from Madras, dating to the 18th century, with one depicting the plants of Tamilnadu with local names in the Armenian script. In Georgia's State Museum, the Virgin Mary sits cross-legged on a lotus, while in Penjikent, Tajikistan, Shiva and Parvati in high boots sit astride a bull. In the Swiss flag, the white cross on a red background is associated with the martyr St Maurice, a 4th century black African from North Egypt, while the coronation mantle, worn by 48 Roman Emperors and Kings, was adorned with Arabic script mentioning the date of its manufacture, 528 Hijra, and praising the king, Roger II. Punjabi folk tales have heroes from Khiva and Bokhara, even as Uzbek and Tajik tales have characters from Kashmir. Sheikh Muinuddin Chishti studied in Bokhara and Samarkand, while Kumarajiva travelled to China to set up a translation centre for Buddhist texts.

And then there are the languages which are waiting to be tapped for words that will reveal their long journeys, concealed histories, stunning revelations and quirky transformations. In North Kerala there is an Arabic Malayalam with 40 per cent Arabic words transmitted over centuries of cultural exchange, whereas in India's northeast, Assam, 600 years of Ahom Thai rule has enriched Assamese with Thai and Chinese terms. The name of the Afghan city, Kandahar, is a derivative of Alexander. The Thai name, Chotima, is linked to the Hindi word for light ('jyotirmoy'), and not to 'little mother', and Angkor (of Angkor Wat fame) is a derivative of '*nagar*' (town in Hindi). Linguistic creativity continues to abound today. The word '*karma*' has acquired new connotations in the American idiom, including 'karma parking' (for those lucky enough to find parking space) and 'karma boomerang'. Closer to home, quirky Francofied names are in vogue, such as the banner on a smart tourist bus on a Delhi street: 'Le Travels to India', and Le Grand Dhaaba, an eatery, on the highway. Meanwhile in Russian, a new English word, 'chat', has entered from the Internet and acquired a Russian declension: I *chatuyu*, You *chatuesh*, He/she *chatuet*, etc.

We continue to live in a fascinating world of cross-cultural interweaves. These myriads of interconnections stretching back in time engulf our daily lives, yet often we are either unaware of them or overlook them due to our conditioning and ingrained notions. This was the case with me — growing up in two countries, India and the erstwhile USSR. While the exposure did indeed widen my cultural horizons, I also imbibed and internalized many standard sacrosanct European cultural models from both Indian and Soviet schools and university textbooks. They had played a significant role in the way I perceived the world around me, including the neighbouring cultures with whom India shared a long history. Yet I was fortunate. Over time, my extensive travels, teaching and research work brought me to experience the most diverse cultures. I followed the trails of the many cultural criss-crossings through space and time, discovering their hidden interlinks and synergies. Many entrenched assumptions were turned upside down and this prompted a reappraisal of what had been imbibed and what ignored. The richness of diverse worlds and the cross-cultural reciprocity provided me with an alternative framework of reference. It enabled me to revise and de-centre my perceptions, but importantly, to rejoice in these discoveries all of which I want to share in this book.

This work, then, explores the overlapping and intermingling of cultures as well as the immense cultural diversity across countries and continents. This exploration inevitably questions any notions of higher or lower cultures, and civilized or uncivilized peoples. Indeed it questions the very concept of superiority amongst peoples. Each community, no matter where it is located on the globe, is unique and the differences are reflected in the multiple layers of culture, but no layer is more authentic than any other. Facets of culture, like travelling metaphors, are transformed and can acquire another meaning as they adapt to different cultures and locations. Perceptions of another culture are often through one's own cultural yardsticks and conditioning. Conversely, a dialogue between two cultures prompts us to examine our own cultural practices, many of which we take for granted. In other words, when people from another culture put questions to our culture, we begin reflecting on ours.

Apart from narrating cross-cultural encounters, this book also discusses how various democratic and non-democratic governments and organizations have attempted to conceal cross-cultural influences by inventing superiority, purity, and authenticity of cultures and civilizations to the detriment of others. Yet cross-culture pollination, an ongoing process, always reveals itself through the ignored cracks of history.

Open interaction and the constant cross-flow of peoples, ideas, objects, language, music, food and much else has always existed between all cultures. This has been catalystic, and notions of exclusiveness, authenticity and roots are questionable, to say the least.

India, like a sponge, has forever absorbed and continues to absorb a bewildering array of influences from outside, including those from the recent avalanche of the West. Yet India is no exception because every culture has been and continues to be porous. The pen-name of the Japanese detective fiction writer is Edogawa Rampo, the Japanese rendering of Edgar Allen Poe, who inspired him. Consider Indonesia, today primarily a country with a predominant Muslim population but with common Sanskritized names: Sukarno (Su karma — good deeds), Veera and Susila. One of the most imposing statues of a seated Ganesha is located near Yogya Jakarta. In nearby Cambodia the 12th century majestic Vishnu temple of Angkor Wat is embellished with exquisitely carved bas relief panels, each 50 to 60 metres long, depicting scenes from Indian mythology: the Churning of the Ocean between the Devas and Asuras; the battle at Kurukshetra between the Pandavas and

Kauravas; battle scenes from the Ramayana and panels devoted to Vishnu and Krishna. In a different location, Van Gogh, with other Impressionist painters as well as the Art Nouveau movement in Europe are all unimaginable without the influence of Japanese wood-cut prints of the artists Hiroshige and Hokusai. Nor can we imagine Picasso's Cubist work without the influence of African masks, or Matisse without his Persian, Moroccan and Asian colours, textile and carpet designs. The Modern Theatre of Bertolt Brecht was deeply influenced by the post-revolutionary Russian Theatre movement of Vsevolod Meyerhold, who in turn was in-debted for his ground-breaking innovations to Chinese theatre. Alexander Tairov, another Russian trendsetter of modern the-atre, was indebted to the *Natyashastra*, the ancient Sanskrit trea-tise on drama.

The contributions made by writers and intellectuals of non-European and mixed descent to European literature and culture are not confined to the recent past but go back many centuries. Apuleius (AD 120-170), who wrote the novel *The Golden Ass*, was from present-day Algeria; Terence (190-158 BC), acknowledged as one of the most eloquent Roman dramatist of comedies in Latin, came from Carthage (Tunisia); Publilius Syrus (1st century BC), well-known for his pithy sayings in Latin including 'It is better to learn late than never', was a Syrian; while Aesop was, as his name suggests, an Ethiopian. The European Renaissance was pro-foundly inspired by the Moorish contributions emanating from their presence for 800 years in Spain, just as the Internet today has been influenced by America.

We have been led to believe that African history begins with the European 'discoveries', yet it was the Africans who discovered Europe and ruled parts of Europe for centuries, even though efforts were made later to erase the memory of these links and to pro-ject the European civilization as a direct offshoot of the Greek and Roman ones. The Greeks, far from being a pure, self-created civilization had been deeply influenced by many neighbouring cultures including the Egyptian and the Persian, all of whom had a profound impact on Roman culture too. Libyan, Tunisian and Syrian Roman Emperors were not exceptions. Even in later times, illustrious families of Europe were ruled by people of mixed blood. The first Duke of the Medici family of Florence, famous for its patronage during the Renaissance, was Alessandro de Medici, the son of an African woman and the future Pope Clement VII. John IV and John VI of Portugal had distinct African features.

Nations have long tried to whitewash and sanitize their cultural histories and links by reinventing a new history. Europeans are not exceptional in wanting to obliterate inconvenient memories. In 1989 I met a young Chinese teacher in Moscow. She was in the first batch on a fellowship to the Soviet Union after a gap of nearly 30 years. Conversing with her, I was shocked to learn that she had never heard of either Confucius or Lao Tse. The Russians too erased the memory of their strong ties with the Turkic people in their textbooks, yet the Russian language reveals a different reality. A great number of their statesmen and intellectuals had Turkic blood, amongst them were Leo Tolstoy, Ivan Turgenev, the historian Karamzin, and the poet Anna Akhmatova.

Where are these pure races, pure cultures and languages, local dress and food?

Today the velocity of cultural mobility has increased. High-speed travel and globalization have catalyzed us into re-examining our entrenched notions. When McDonalds, which prided itself on its standard meat-burger, had to adapt its menu to the Indian palate and serve a vegetarian burger for the first time to safeguard its profitability, it was time to re-examine what constitutes national cuisine. In the Latin Quarter of Paris, the fastest selling pizzas are those made by an Indian who deftly wraps some stuffing into a roti. Inevitably this fast pace of foreign exchanges should have led many self-proclaimed superior cultures to re-evaluate their own history and accept pluralism and multiculturalism.

In 2002, on his 200th birth anniversary, the body of Alexandre Dumas Pere, one of the most prolific and widely read French writers, the author of *The Three Musketeers* and *The Count of Monte Cristo,* was exhumed and shifted to the Pantheon in the company of the graves of 60 luminaries. Accepting underlying racial prejudice for the fact that Dumas' grandmother was an Afro-Caribbean,

President Chiraq acknowledged that finally a wrong had been righted. In 2009, his successor, President Nicolas Sarkozy, uneasy with the notion of multiculturalism, set up a parliamentary committee to decide on the merits of wearing a *burqa* in public. Yet it was not so long ago that the French and English colonialists had forced an all-concealing Christian moral dress code on their colonies, and topless women, for instance, were directed to wear blouses. At London's Heathrow airport, a cleaning lady of Punjabi descent lost her job for sporting a nose-ring. In 2008, Malaysia's top Islamic body banned the practice of yoga for Muslims as being un-Islamic, whereas in the United Kingdom two churches banned yoga classes for toddlers on their premises, branding it as un-Christian. However, yoga is also the cash cow for some Americans who are registering various patents for several postures. The US Patent and Trademark Office has granted 150 yoga-related copyrights and 134 patents on yoga accessories. Some non-resident Indians living in America have gone to court to ban the depiction of Ganesha holding a beer mug — oblivious that the most popular items on sale at Diwali in north Indian bazaars are the replicas of Ganesha, Laxmi and other deities with Chinese features that have been imported from China.

There are growing attempts at cultural policing. Yet, connectivity is what matters, not fears of some imaginary phantoms that are reactivated and fostered periodically. Perhaps it is constructive to listen to those who do not have the privilege of being heard, and whose wisdom is overlooked. Only then can we appreciate the multiple realities co-existing, interacting and constantly enriching our world.

'Mohammad formed the marriage procession and Brahma set up the posts (of the marriage canopy).

The Maids of heaven sang songs of rejoicing and fairies brought the henna.

The Panj Pir performed the ceremony and Khwaja (Khizar) was witness.

Hir and Ranjha met together and God was favourable to them'

Aap Mohammad janj charia, Brahma Bedi gadai,

Ralke huran mangal gavian, pariyan mehndi lai.

Panjan Piran ne kalime parh lie, Khaja bhare ogahi.

Hir Ranjha da mela ho gaya, phirian rabb rajai.

This quotation is from the folk version of the famous love story of Heer and Ranjha and their wedding. It was published in the 1884 edition of *The Legends of Panjab*, collected by R.C. Temple, from local bards. The entire tale abounds in this syncretism. When Heer is abducted by King Adali, Ranjha plays his flute in despair.

'The sound of the flute reached to Makka and a company of 70 saints came up.

The sound of the flute reached to Multan and the Five Saints came in majesty.

The sound of the flute brought the Mother, the Goddess (Durga), on her lion to Ranjha.

At the sound of the flute came (Sakhi) Sarwar the Warrior, caracoling on (his mare) Kakki.

At the sound of the flute came Hanuman, the leader with his army.

The army cut down the garden of Adali and left not a tree remaining.'

Adali frees Heer and when Ranjha sounded his conch, Indra caused rain. Now they were properly married and 'Ranjha took Heer and took the road to Makka'.

A number of essays in this collection were published in 2006 in *Foreign Exchange* in the OpEd page of *Daily Times*, Lahore. Subsequently, some of these appeared in Indian newspapers in English and regional languages. Others were translated into foreign languages. Since the *Daily Times* is also an online paper, many have appeared on numerous websites and blogs in Armenian, Georgian, Thai, Russian and Kazakh. A few of the essays in this collection appeared in the magazine, *Herald* , in 2008–2009 in Karachi.

In an age when specialization has led to the compartmentalization of various disciplines, this work is an attempt to break down these barriers and bring together seemingly disparate elements, all of which are interlinked. The sequence of chapters remains as it appeared in the newspaper and magazine. This may seem odd, but clubbing them by subject would only reinforce the very compartmentalization which has been the bane of researchers and which has resulted in hermetically sealed cultural constructs.

I would like to thank Najam Sethi and the editorial staff of *Daily Times*, specially Ejaz Haidar, as well as Arifa Noor, the Editor of the *Herald,* and Fareeha Rafique. I am indebted also to the countless readers who were most generous in their appreciation and gave me invaluable inputs. And then of course, there is my family, the fellow-travellers Romi and Martand. Their witticisms, criticism, Queen's English, puns and laughter ensured the progress of this journey.

❇

The Black Virgin

◉

In 1999 the Mayor of New York, Rudolph Giuliani, tried to prevent the opening of an art exhibition at the city-funded Brooklyn Museum of Art. The Mayor was offended by one of the exhibits depicting the Virgin Mary and threatened to freeze the annual funds for the Museum if it went ahead with the show. Catholic organizations labelled the work sacrilegious and obscene. The art community and the American Civil Liberties Union in contrast came out in support of the exhibit. The controversy snowballed. The Museum Director defended the exhibition, went to Court and won the case. The debate ensured serpentine lines to the box office while devout Catholics prayed and chanted outside the Museum.

But there were latent undertones to all this. Chris Ofili, the painter, is British born, British educated, a British citizen, recipient of the prestigious Turner Award and an avowed Roman Catholic. However he is black and his Virgin Mary is also black and decorated with elephant dung — a threat to powerful cultural prejudices.

So, which image of the Virgin Mary is authentic? Does European iconography possess the only authentic representations? What about the images of the Copts or the Assyrian Christians — societies which had adopted Christianity before Rome?

The Egyptian Coptic church is the oldest of them all. St. Mark, the Apostle, began preaching in Egypt in AD 35, whereas St. Thomas is said to have preached and converted in Iraq 40 years after Christ. Christian converts existed in Palestine, Lebanon, Syria and Persia in the first century, followed a little while later in Armenia and Georgia. In North East Africa the Coptic influence percolated to the Ethiopians and Nubians. The depiction of Mary was wide-spread and, understandably, in these regions, Mary is not a blue-eyed blonde. In fact, I have even come across a Virgin Mary seated in *padma asana* on a lotus in Georgia's State Museum!

But let us return to Europe where Christianity was officially adopted some 400 years after Christ. Although initially the church in Rome forbade any type of imagery, there were numerous shrines all over Europe where the image of the Virgin Mary was wor-shipped. These images are said to have been discovered between the 10th and 12th centuries. How was she depicted? Believe it or not — she is black! Her features, in most instances, are non-European. And ironically, most of these images are located in Catholic churches in France, Italy, Spain, Portugal, Germany, Austria and Switzerland [**Plates 1 and 2**]. I am not out to distort history but the veneration for the Black Madonna never ceased, and she continues to be worshipped to this day.

France alone has 300 documented Black Madonna shrines — the largest number, including the famous 13th century statue in the Chartres Cathedral. Spain has 50 (including one in Montserrat near Barcelona), Italy , 30, and 19 in Germany. Poland's most sacred site is the shrine of the Charna (black) Madonna of Czestochowa — the protector of Poland. Her icon is said to have been made by St. Luke. Over 30 million people visit her shrine annually.

Initially the Catholic church did not acknowledge the presence of the many Black Madonnas in their churches, but later explained away the 'black' colour' as a deposit caused by the soot residue from the votive candles and smoking incense. Yet it was unable to explain why only the various faces and hands had succumbed to the soot deposits while the clothes had retained their bright colours, or why many of the images had African-like features.

Interest around the Black Virgin or Madonna has grown tremen-dously. Explanatory theories have been advanced claiming the origins of this cult back to the Egyptian Goddess, Isis, who was venerated all over the Roman empire. It is believed by some that with the advent of Christianity in Europe the image of Isis with

Horus in her lap was transformed into Mary and Christ. Still others claim that the dark image represents Mary Magdalene holding in her arms the son of Christ. Many of these Black Madonnas are said to possess miraculous healing powers and so continue to attract thousands of devotees annually.

The most intriguing image, however, is in Les Saintes Maries de la Mer church in France. Here the Black Madonna is venerated as the patron saint of the Gypsies. Every year they congregate from all parts of Europe on 24th or 25th May and pay homage to the image they call, interestingly, Kali Sara. (Kali as Durga, Kali as in Black or both?) She is first dressed in new attire and then her relics are taken to the sea where they are purified through immersion and carried back to the Church. So, which of all these Madonnas is the authentic one? Or are they all equally authentic, none more so than the other?

Travelling Buddha

O ne of our neighbours in the Kangra valley where we live is an American, who was a Buddhist lama in a Tibetan monastery in France for fourteen years. That is, till he fell in love with one of his students and decided to get married. Another neighbour is a Swiss Buddhist, who is painting eight giant size *thangkas* for a Buddhist ceremony. One does not have to convince anyone that Buddhism has been one of the fastest growing spiritual movements in the 20th century, thanks primarily to the charismatic Dalai Lama. But how many people are aware that a long time ago, before the advent of modern technology and fast travel, Buddha was 'adopted' by Christianity and is even today revered as a Christian Saint!

If Buddhism travelled eastwards incorporating elements of local religions and beliefs, its journey westwards was no less remarkable. The story of Gautama Siddhartha underwent a series of transformations in Persian, then Arabic, then Georgian, from which it was translated into Greek, surprisingly, only in the 11th century. In the Georgian and Greek versions of Buddha's life the Christian element dominates and Buddha converts to Christianity. Translations and adaptations into major European languages were carried out from the Greek version. The tale of Buddha or *Iosaaf* was the first printed book in Bulgaria after the advent of Christianity. The Russian translation dates back to the latter half of the 11th or early 12th century. There are over 140 versions of Buddha's stories in thirty languages. He is variously known as Josaphat, Jasaph, Iosaaf, Ioasaph, Iasaph, Joasaph and Yudasaf — all names, strangely enough, derivatives from the Middle Persian *Budsaif*, which in turn is from *Bodhisattva*.

The Christian version of Buddha's life story concerns the Indian King Abenner (also Avenier) of the 3rd or 4th century who persecuted his Christian subjects. An astrologer predicted that Abenner's son Josaphat would one day become a Christian. Consequently the King confined his son within the palace. But one day, Josaphat happened to venture out and saw the misery surrounding him [**Plate 3**]. On this journey he met the Christian hermit, Barlaam who convinced him to convert to Christianity, 'the true faith'. Josaphat attained enlightenment through his love for Jesus Christ. Later Abenner also converted to Christianity and abdicated the throne. Josaphat governed for a while, then travelled to the desert, found his mentor Barlaam and spent the rest of his days 'in holiness'. After their deaths their bodies were brought back to India and buried in the very church Josaphat had built prior to his departure from home.

In the 16th-century Russian version, fifty-five wise men appear at the time of Buddha's/Iosaaf's birth and the eldest of them predicts that the child would embrace Christianity. In this version Varlaam, the hermit, enters the palace disguised as a merchant and promises to show Buddha a rare jewel. When asked to produce it he relates one 'Christian' (read *Jataka*) fable after another, and thereby convinces the prince of the merits of becoming a Christian. The story *Varlaam and Iosaaf, the Indian Prince* was, for centuries, one of the most popular tales in Russia.

For the Catholic Church, 27 November is celebrated as the day of Saint Josaphat and Barlaam, in the Greek calendar it is 26 August and for the Russian Orthodoxy, 14th of November is the day of *Iosaaf*. Not far from Moscow is the famous Izmailov island, where the church of *Iosaaf* (or Buddha!) was built in 1678. Medieval Christian illustrations of Josaphat/ Buddha depict him in European attire. The links with India disappeared in the sands of space and time.

In 1651 Engelbert Kaempfer , a former diplomat in the service of the Swedish King, and later an employee of the Dutch East India Company, visited Siam (present-day Thailand). His response to the Buddha is given in his book of travelogue, *A Description of the Kingdom of Siam*:

> The Siamites represent the first Teacher of their Paganism in their Temples, in the figure of a Negro sitting, of prodigious size, his hair curl'd, the skin black, ...

Kaempfer feels that the South Asians are a confused lot because the

> Siamites call the Country of his nativity Lanca....The Ceylonese themselves call the Country of his nativity Macca desia, meaning by it the Kingdom of Siam....The Chinese and Japanese pretend that this saint, and the Doctrine he reveal'd, had their origin in the Country of Magatta, or as the Japanese call it, Tensik Magatta Kokf, that is the Heavenlandish Magatta, which according to their description and opinion is the Continent of India...

It was left to the former diplomat to 'straighten this confusion'. Buddha was

> no Asiatick, or Indian, but some Egyptian Priest of note, probably of Memphis, and a Moor, who with his brethren being expell'd their native Country, brought the Egyptian Religion into the Indies, and propagated it there...

Yet another legend is created.

Coffee

◙

In today's world of instant weight loss, instant hair growth, instant nirvana and instant coffee, there remains a dwindling community of coffee lovers whose eyes light up at the mention of 'Turkish coffee': dense black coffee in tiny cups, the flavour of freshly ground coffee beans lingering in one's mouth. Turkish coffee evokes images of the hookah that accompanies it, or the sweets Turkish Delight, which you nibble at as you sip your coffee. Your mind wanders to medieval Istanbul and its coffee houses described in Orhan Pamuk's novel, *My Name is Red*; meeting places of commoners and miniaturist painters, Sufi dervishes and writers; the art of brewing coffee, the intricate ceremony associated with it; the different categories of sweetness the Turks assign to it; the anecdotes linked to coffee and the Turkish proverb, 'coffee should be black as hell, strong as death and sweet as love'; brides who were earlier chosen on the basis of their coffee making skills; alternately wives who were within their legal rights in seeking a divorce if their husbands did not provide them with their daily portion of coffee. And then you come across an article, *Coffee and Democracy* by Aziz Nesin, the renowned Turkish satirist:

> There are two items our country does not produce: coffee and demo-cracy. We import them from abroad. What to do? Coffee does not grow here and that's that! Nothing suits it: neither the climate, nor the water, nor the soil. That is why we gave up on coffee [cultivation].

So how is it then that when we order 'Turkish coffee' many of us take for granted that this coffee we are about to consume originates in Turkey? Actually, a particular way of brewing coffee is known as Turkish coffee. Just as with the turkey bird, coffee became associated with the country — the conduit or port of transit to Europe.

Coffee was known to have grown wild in present-day Ethiopia. Its inhabitants harvested and consumed the berries and leaves way back in the 6th century. Subsequently it spread to the Arab lands, and was first cultivated in Yemen in the 14th century. Then began its journeys — Egypt in the early 16th century, Syria and Turkey. Baba Budan is said to have brought the seeds from Yemen on his journey home from Mecca in the early 17th century and planted them in south India, from where the Dutch, a hundred years later, transported the saplings to their colony in Indonesia. Coffee percolated down into Europe through Venice, Marseilles and Vienna. By 1650 it arrived in England, where in less than 30 years, 300 coffee houses sprang up.

But not everyone took an instant liking for this beverage in Europe. The Dutchman Olearius who visited 17th-century Persia writes

> They drink with their tobacco a certain black water which they call cahwa [coffee] made of a fruit brought out of Egypt and which is in color like ordinary wheat, and in taste like Turkish wheat, and is of the bigness of a little bean. They fry (or rather burn) it in an iron pan without any liquor, beat it to powder, and boiling with fair water, they make this drink thereof which hath as it were the taste of a burnt crust and is not pleasant to the palate.

Olearius was unaware of the variety of flavours enjoyed in the Middle East where coffee can be spiced with cloves, cinnamon and cardamom. In fact, I became addicted to coffee with cardamom in my student days thanks to some Lebanese friends, and quite by chance discovered that cardamom is a natural decaffeinating agent.

On its journeys the Arabic kahwa (or qahva) became kahve in Turkish and thus caffè in Italian and the French café for coffee and coffee houses; coffee in English; cafeteria — coffee store). Some opine that the Arabic kahva could be a derivative of the coffee-growing area Kaffa in Ethiopia where, incidentally, coffee is known as buno, and in Yemen, bunn.

The Kashmiri word *kahwa* is also a derivative of Arabic, yet the ingredients that go into the making of Kashmiri *kahwa* are not coffee beans but green tea leaves along with cinnamon and cardamom. Although it is called coffee it is actually tea. The word remains but the content has changed.

Meanwhile food and beverages can also be roped into national politics. In the divided island of Cyprus, if one is in the Greek Cypriot part of the island one has to refrain from asking for Turkish coffee. Since the partition of the country it is now referred to as Cypriot coffee. In the Turkish Cypriot part of the island you can still enjoy the same coffee, with its flavours and name intact.

Cultural Baggage

◫

On a Sunday morning I walked into St. John's Cathedral in Valetta, the capital of Malta. The church was packed for the morning service. I found a seat in the last row and let my gaze wander over the opulent Baroque interior. Moments later the priest arrived in regal vestments. He climbed the few steps to the pulpit, adjusted his robes, then peered through his spectacles at the congregation and loudly uttered the first word, '*Allah!*'

That one word filled the interior, floated up to the ornate vaulted dome and bounced back to resonate loudly in my ears. Did I let out a gasp? A quick furtive look around assured me of the opposite. Everyone was engrossed in prayer. As for me, unable any longer to concentrate on anything, I tiptoed out.

How many misconceptions we carry in our cultural baggage. I had always associated 'Allah' with Arabic, and hence with Islam. Never could I have imagined this word being uttered in a Roman Catholic church, built for the Crusaders. And yet, what, after all, is 'Allah'? It is 'God', pure and simple in Arabic. I was still pondering over that word as I approached a monument. It read, *Il Monument ta' l-Ghassedju l-Kbir*, or The Great Siege Monument — a mixture of Italian and Arabic. I then recalled a similar cultural fusion in the Cathedral where an eight-pointed star is depicted — each point representing one of the Romance languages that made up the Knights Order of St. John; yet the church service is in a Semitic language.

The Fatimid Arabs ruled Malta from 870 AD for about 200 years. They established their capital Medina (Mdina), introduced dhow boats and left behind their language. Like other Mediterranean

cultures, Malta is a genetic melting pot of the various nationalities who overran it as conquerors or traders: Phoenicians (from
present-day Lebanon, Syria, Palestine and Israel), Greeks, Tunisians,
Romans, Aghlabid Arabs from North Africa, Normans, Italians,
Spaniards, French and British. Today the Maltese could be mistaken
for Sicilians or Arabs. Their food is Sicilian, their laws — British,
their script — Latin, and religion — Roman Catholic.

I recall another episode which, in a similar manner, dislodged my
set ideas. Some years later we were in Palestine in mid-December
and decided that Christmas eve at Christ's birthplace was a must.
Haven't we all grown up with the familiar images of the Nativity:
the Christmas tree covered in snow, the cuddly, fair, pink-cheeked
baby Jesus in his crypt with a distinctly European looking mother
Mary?

On arrival in Bethlehem we were in for a cultural shock. Instead of
snow we were confronted with nothing but sand which had even
found its way into the town's main square. The only vegetation in
sight were the gnarled olive trees. Moreover, the crypt where Jesus
is said to have been born is enclosed in a Greek Orthodox church.
This church lends its space to the Catholics on the night of 24
December for their Midnight Mass. Orthodox Christians and the
Copts celebrate Christ's birthday two weeks later, on 7 January,
and the Armenian Church even later, on 19 January. And so it goes
on and on. All that remained of my conditioning was the cherubic
plaster of Paris baby Jesus being sold in the Bethlehem bazaar by
Palestinian shopkeepers (incidentally, not only is this town Christian and Palestinian, 90 per cent of the Christians of the Holy Land
are the Palestinian).

There was wonderful choir singing that night in the main Bethlehem
square. Groups from across the globe had flown in to perform
Christmas carols. Initially bodies swayed gently to the familiar
melodies while some onlookers tapped their feet to the rhythms.
The audience really came alive when the last but one choir began
singing. It was from India.

Was I dreaming or was there really a Sardar in the choir?

I nudged my son. He smiled and nodded. By now the entire public
was clapping to the rhythm of the music. Some people stood up

and began to dance. They set the mood. Within minutes everyone was clapping, dancing and singing — such was the contagious rhythm and sound of the Indian choir's carols.

I met the group a few days later. We were on the same flight to Bombay.

'Did you manage to see the crypt that night?' I asked one of them.

'No, the crowd was too big but we saw it the previous day. In any case, on Christmas night the Christians should have the first priority to enter the crypt...'

'Aren't you all Christians?'

The young man smiled. *'We have everyone in our group — Christians and non-Christians. You must have noticed our Sardar ji. Then there are Maharashtrians, Parsees, Punjabis, Gujaratis, Goans, just about everyone. We love singing so we joined this choir in Bombay.'*

Words' Worth

An Uzbek friend was excitedly showing me the trousseau she had collected for her daughter. Shimmering lengths of fabric were brought out of the chest. Some were velvety looking, with golden embroidery, others with sequins. I had never come across this range of fabrics in the shops of Samarkand or Tashkent.

'*Where did you buy all this from?*' I couldn't help asking.

'*Dubai*', came the pat reply.

'*I didn't know you'd been to Dubai!*' I exclaimed.

'*I haven't. But I placed my order with those who travelled to the UAE.*'

Our conversation took place at a time when travel restrictions had just been lifted and chartered flights from the erstwhile Soviet Union to international destinations for 'business' purposes were on the rise.

I persisted with my queries. '*How would <u>they</u> know what you required?*'

'*Very simple. I told them to bring me back two metres of black Stephanie, five metres each of Caroline and Brooke, some Macey...*'

'*Are those the names of the fabrics?*'

'*Yes*', Shahista smiled, '*they're all based on the characters of* The Bold and the Beautiful.'

'*Wha-a-t?*'

'*Well, we had no idea what these fabrics were. We'd never seen any-thing like this before. Just then this American serial was being aired on TV. So the women decided to name the textiles themselves….*'

'*Are many people familiar with these names in Samarkand?*'

'*Why only Samarkand?! Everyone in Uzbekistan regularly orders these fabrics from the Middle East. We've also got fabric names like chameleon, dollar and Marianne (from another TV serial).*'

A TV soap opera in one country acquires a totally different usage in another culture for defining a cultural entity in a third country.

Cross-cultural transformations along their journeys take on a magical quality. At times some logic seems to exist, at other times it needs the likes of a Sherlock Holmes to make head or tail of the adventures.

Take the turkey bird. It was presumably brought to India by the Portuguese from Peru. Thus, in some south Indian languages it is called *peru*. Then begin the bird's travels to northern regions. Before long this bird became associated with India in regions as far apart as Afghanistan, Russia and Basque. Could it be because our subcontinent had always been linked to exotic and strange looking creatures? In Afghanistan and Central Asia it is called *hindi*, in the Arab lands, *diiq hindi*, or Indian rooster. In the Azeri language spoken by the peoples of Azerbaijan and parts of Iran, it is called *hindishga* (from India) and in Turkey, *hindi*. Likewise, in Russian the word is *indyuk* for the male and *indeika* (from India) for the female, and similarly, in Polish, Ukrainian and Bulgarian it is *indyk*. In France the bird is called *dinde* or *dindon* (from India), in Germany *indianische Henn*, in the Basque language, *indioilar* or *indioilo* (India rooster, India hen), in the Catalan language, *gall dindi* (cock from India). The bird's adventures continued. From Turkey the bird branched off to Egypt where it became known as *dik-rumi* ('rumi' in those days referred to Turkey), thus Turkish fowl, and from Egypt presumably to Macedonia where it is called *misir* and *misirka* (the Turkish and Arabic name for Egypt being *misr*). The Turks must have carried this bird straight to England, bypassing France, hence the name — turkey. And finally to Portugal where the bird is called *peru*. But more confusion follows.

The scientific name given to this huge fowl is *Meleagris gallopavo*; *Meleagris* (generic name) in Greek means guinea fowl — a bird about 53–58 cm in size (the turkey is 117 cm). The species name in Latin is *gallopavo*: *gallus* (cock) plus *pavo* (peafowl) — the species name for peacock. Translated into everyday language, we get a cock-like, peacock guinea fowl.

The inevitable question is why the bird's common name has no links to its Spanish one — *pavo* — for it was the Spaniards who brought it back from Mexico to Europe around 1524. Moreover, it was the Spaniards who colonised Peru and Mexico, not the Portuguese. The turkey had been domesticated by the Mayans (of southern Mexico and northern Central America) and Aztecs (of central Mexico) over 2000 years ago. In the Nahualt language of the Aztecs it was known as *huexolotlin*. The Mayans called it *cutz*. Other local names for it in Latin America are *guajolote*, *totole*, *chompipe* and *chunto*.

Oddly enough, in some of the Scandinavian languages the bird's name is linked to Calicut. In Dutch it is *kalkoense hahn*, in Danish, *kalkun*, in Swedish, *kalkon*, *kalkun* and *kalkkuna* in Estonian and Finnish, and another German name for it is *Calecutishe Hahn*.

And finally, not to be missed is *shutar murg* in Hindi and Punjabi. *Shutar* is a derivative of the Persian word for camel (*shotor*). The camel cock?

Batata Aloo

◻

Can we visualise our sedate Prime Minister sporting a broccoli flower in the buttonhole and his equally dignified wife decorating her hair with it for the cause of encouraging the Indian farmer to cultivate this *angrezi gobi?* The sub-continent being what it is, the only thing that would proliferate and flourish will be the jokes.

Today's politicians might lack a sense of humour and not appreciate the advantages of this nutritious plant, but in earlier days, members of the French royal family certainly were not squeamish about adorning themselves with vegetables. Louis XVI and his wife proudly sported the potato flower just to encourage potato cultivation. And it worked! This potato buttonhole diplomacy, reinforced with Marie Antoinette's coiffeur a la potato flowers, succeeded where Louis XVI' s two predecessors had failed despite passing legislation and issuing threats. Earlier, faced with a popular uprising over escalating bread prices, Louis XIV on the advice of his botanists passed a decree on the imperative of cultivating potatoes. It misfired. His successor decided that the fault lay with the government's insensitivity to the French language. The 'crude' South American term 'batata' was elevated in stature and received a regal nomenclature — *pomme de terre* or, the apple of the earth… again to no avail. Apple or not, the French peasant wasn't interested.

This lump of starch, which today is taken for granted in nearly 250 countries as a basic diet, has had a turbulent history of acceptance. It had to fight its way inch by inch to get on to dining tables.

For nearly 200 years the European peasant resisted all government attempts to impose potato cultivation, convinced that this bland, tasteless tuber was the cause of leprosy, sexual debility, syphilis and early death. How were they to know that this tuber, brought back by the Spaniards from Peru, had been grown and consumed for centuries by the Incas, who were adept at drying and storing this root which came in a large variety of colours and shapes.

In those early times, little was known of this imported item. One Elizabethan English enthusiast decided to introduce it to the aristocracy. He made the fatal error of cooking just the leaves and berries and throwing away the ugly misshapen tubers. The result was food poisoning of the royal guinea pigs. Potato vanished off the English menu for a long time.

The struggle for acceptance did not succeed any better in neighbouring Prussia. Frederick the Great passed a potato cultivation order in 1774. The citizens of the town of Kolberg responded: 'The things have neither smell, nor taste, not even the dogs will eat them, so what use are they to us?' Frederick threatened to cut off the nose and ears of those who refused to comply. His obsession with potatoes seeped into Russia where, Catherine the Great, also a German, passed a similar order but to no avail. In Russia the church too resisted and termed it the 'devil's weed'. Revolts were met with repression.

Finally, in the mid 19th century, after two failed wheat harvests and a famine, the Russian peasants eventually turned to potato cultivation. Within 50 years the volume of potato cultivation rose 400 times. Today it is difficult to imagine Russian cuisine without potatoes. The best vodka is of course made from potatoes.

And then there are the Irish who consider the potato plant as the Queen of the garden. They even get lyrical over it: 'It is easy to halve a potato where there is love', or ' two things in this world are too serious to jest about, potatoes and matrimony'. The colonised Irish peasants, impoverished and dispossessed of their land by the English, were forced into growing potato as a mono crop on their tiny land holdings. By the mid-19th century the Irish had become completely dependent on potatoes as their staple diet.

Three major potato crop failures in four years (between 1845 and 1850) led to famine and the death of half the population, widespread unrest, followed by the exodus to North America. It was, ironically the Irish and Scots who brought the potato back to the American continent.

Stranger things were to occur once potato cultivation had taken off in Europe. Prussia and Austria were engaged in a stalemated Potato War in 1778. With neither side winning the two armies plundered each other's potato fields in a bid to starve each other to death.

Brought by the Portuguese in the 17th century to our subcontinent, we fortunately absorbed this tuber without coercion or threat. Instead of boiling it like Europeans, we transformed it with spices: *aloo tikki, aloo bhujia, aloo chaat, dum aloo, aloo dosa, batata vada* etc., in the north calling it by the Persian word *aloo* meaning 'plum'. In the south it remains *batata*.

✳

7

Halo! Halo!

◳

Occasionally cultural assimilations emerge out of the most unexpected bends and corners of history. I would like to share what for me came as a surprise, but could well be a known fact to others.

We were standing in front of some medieval 13th–15th century Italian paintings in the Getty Museum. Suddenly I was pulled by the sleeve and literally dragged to a painting in one corner by my companion.

'Look carefully, do you notice anything?'

I looked. It was a painting of the Virgin Mary and Christ. Nice. Nothing special.

'Examine the halo! And the dress, the border…'

'So?!'

And then my eyes focussed. There was Arabic script all over the surfaces — in the halo, along the border of the dress and on the sleeves of the revered Christian figures. I rushed to the next work and it was the same.

'This can't be true'; I exclaimed.

Yet there it was, what, a while ago, had been an innocuous design in the paintings of Gentile da Fabriano, Fra Angelico and Gherardo Starnina was definitely Arabic script.

Later I looked up websites and albums of Italian art, rummaged through art books and chanced upon an old article in *Aramco* magazine, which corroborated my observations. The Italian painters did indeed resort to these designs, which are known as mock Arabic calligraphy. What irony. Christian divinities and saints with Kufic lettering in their halos and dresses.

One version is that the Crusaders returned from the Middle East bringing back booty, which included rich fabrics with Arabic calligraphy embroidered on them. These inscribed fabrics ended up as altar covers in European churches, or were tailored and altered into liturgical garments. Conferring robes (*khilats* in Turkic) to royalty or visiting dignitaries was an ancient tradition in the East, as was the tradition of adding an inscription on the fabric.

The term *tiraz* ('embroidery' in Persian) was adapted by the Arabs to designate embroidered or woven inscriptions in textiles. Later the meaning extended to weaving workshops.

But the story of these inscriptions does not end with the Crusaders. The coronation mantle of the Norman king Roger II of Sicily has real Arabic script embroidered on the border. It praises the King and states that the mantle was made in the royal workshops of Palermo in 528, by the Islamic calendar, corresponding to 1133. It may be recalled that although Roger's father captured Sicily from the Arabs, the island remained a pluralistic and tolerant society. This beautiful coronation mantle of heavy red silk weighs 11kg and is more than 11 feet wide. Over a 100,000 pearls have been sown into the fabric, which has intricate gold thread embroidery. Two stylised lions on either side of a date palm tree are depicted triumphing over two camels. The design is undoubtedly a mix of Arab, Iranian and Central Asian (with Kazakh appliqué work). The lions signified a victory over the foes, and the date palm tree, a symbol of life. The mantle is now in the custody of the Kunsthistoriche Museum in Vienna [**Plates 4 and 5**].

Significantly, this royal mantle and some other inner garments with Arabic *tiraz* on the borders, and Roger's red silk and calf shoes (with gold thread embroidery, pearls, sapphires and rubies) became the coronation robes for 48 Roman emperors and kings from the year 1220 (when Frederic, Roger's grandson, crowned himself King of Germany) right up to the 18th century. Curious that none of these exalted personalities seemed unduly disturbed by the Arabic origins or the inscriptions.

That might explain how the motif jumps from clothes to paintings. If every Roman emperor wore these clothes at the time of his coronation and perhaps, even for other ceremonial occasions, it would not be long before the painters turned to this 'pattern'. Would that explain the mock Arabic calligraphy on the border of the Bishop Saint in Fra Angelico's 15th century painting *Saint Francis and a Bishop Saint*?

From the 13th to the 16th century numerous Italian painters turned to mock Arabic calligraphy in their works pertaining to Christian themes. They included the mentioned painters, as also Simone Martini (1284–1344) and the Florentine painter Nardo di Cione (1343–65/66). These 'borrowings' are most striking in the works of Gentile da Fabriano, especially in his painting *Adoration of the Magi*, in which, let alone the garments, even the golden halos of the Holy Family are 'embossed' with mock Arabic calligraphy, inspired, according to experts, by the inscriptions on Egyptian and Syrian brass plates inlaid with silver and gold [**Plates 6 and 7**].

My search and discoveries, although exciting, were those of an amateur. There is, undoubtedly, a veritable treasure house of cultural interactions in the throws of rediscovery. Despite the concerted attempts in Europe to 'sanitise' their histories, some assimilations do have the knack of spilling out of ignored cracks and crevices.

8

Tuneful Maladies

◨

Way back in 1956, Soviet leaders Krushchev and Bulganin visited India. A cultural troupe accompanied them and performed at the Regal Cinema, Delhi's largest theatre at the time. That particular show became a favourite family tale repeated to one and all. The Soviet guests had brought a mixed bag of entertainment. The performance commenced with some acrobats followed by clowns. Next came the turn of one of the Soviet Union's leading opera singers. He launched into a well-known aria. The moment the singer raised his voice and held it at a high pitch the audience burst out laughing. The singer turned red, halted and made a second attempt. Now there was pandemonium — laughter, applause and cries of '*Wah, wah!*' The singer was at his wits end. After a third try he gave up and walked off the stage. He had never been so insulted. I doubt if he ever set foot again in India. How was the poor man to know that most of the people in the audience had never heard a Western opera before. No wonder they thought he was continuing the comic antics of the previous performer, the clown.

Years later not much had changed except for a reversal of roles in the realm of music appreciation. Now the scene was Moscow prior to the Indian Festival of 1986. For the opening ceremony the Russian organisers required from their Indian counterparts the programme details. All they were given were the names of leading Indian performers including, M.S.Subbulaxmi.

'*Please understand, we also need the names of the items to be included in the programme brochure.*'

'*That we cannot tell you. It depends on the performer.*'

'*What d' you mean?*'

'*Well, the performers decide which Raga they are going to sing or play at that particular moment.*'

The Russians were totally nonplussed. '*You mean to say we just insert the names of the players in the brochure?*'

'*Yes.*'

'*How many minutes is each performer going to take?*'

'*It can be fifteen minutes, half an hour or even more. It's up to the players. If they get into the mood and connect with the audience there's no stopping them. They can carry on all night...*'

The Russians were aghast. They imagined a fiasco staring them in the face — all because of downright Indian incompetence.

Appreciating foreign, especially classical, music is perhaps the most difficult hurdle to cross. I have Russian Indologist friends who have spent their lives researching various aspects of our subcontinent, but wild horses could not drag them to a Bhimsen Joshi concert.

Was it any different earlier? Lourenco Mexia, the Portuguese missionary in 16th century Japan, was horrified by Japanese music.

> Although they make use of pitch, neither going up nor down, their natural and artificial music is so dissonant and harsh to our ears that it is quite a trial to listen to it for a quarter of an hour; but to please the Japanese we are obliged to listen to it for many hours. They themselves like it so much that they do not think there is anything to equal it in the wide world, and although our music is melodious, it is regarded by them with repugnance.

His colleague, Luis Frois, S.J., was harsher in his comments: 'We consider harmonized music sweet and melodious; in Japan everybody howls together and the effect is simply awful.'

Classical Persian music fared no better for the 19th century English traveller to Persia, Gertrude Bell. She was made to endure 'weird, tuneless' and 'endless wailing' melodies played on a 'stringed instrument'.

On the other hand, Ibrahim ibn Yáqūb, a native of Tortos in 10th century Spain, could not handle Western Music:

> I have never heard worse singing than that of the people of Schleswig. It is a humming that comes out of their throats, like the barking of dogs, but more beastlike.

With such strong emotional reactions to foreign music, can we surmise that music is outside the purview of comprehension or transference? Not really. The process might be slower (especially with regard to classical music), imperceptible perhaps, but on-going. The impact of jazz, the fusion of Spanish, Arab and Gypsy music in Flamenco, the guitar rage all over the world are some examples. Another more striking instance of assimilation that we may take for granted is the army brass band — a British legacy to the ex-colonies. Band music is now an integral part of our official ceremonial functions and Gymkhana Club jamborees. In India brass bands have percolated down to private weddings with their epaulets, uniforms, bugles, drums and melodies. These wedding bands announce their presence by the sheer decibel level of their melodies as they weave their way through the traffic, leading the *baraat* and the bridegroom who sits on a horse, eager to march into the bridal chamber.

❄

9

Candy'd Talk

◙

'There's a reed which makes honey without bees!', exclaimed a bewildered officer in Alexander's army when he chanced upon this strange novelty in India in 327BC. The confusion about honey persisted even a few centuries later: how could it be 'so brittle that it has to be broken between the teeth?' Honey had been the only sweetener in much of Europe till the early 14th century.

Sugarcane, the so-called 'honey reed', is said to have grown in the Pacific islands as far back as 5000 years ago. When and how it travelled to the Indian subcontinent is a matter of conjecture. Some believe the Polynesians brought it to our parts on their journeys. Regardless of its origins, sugarcane has been grown in India for thousands of years and, consequently, our collective sweet tooth is provided with a bewildering variety of sweets! The flight of sugar and sugarcane derivatives from the Indian sub-continent is like a series of boomerang flights — it left our shores only to return to us from all quarters.

Not only did sugar travel, its nomenclature too went on a journey. The history or etymology of the English word 'sugar' is derived from the Sanskrit and north Indian languages — *sharkara* and *shakkar*. This word underwent slight variations as the substance was readily relished on its journeys: from the Persian *shakar* (cultivated there as far back as AD 500) to *sukkar* in Arabic, *shaakhar* in Armenian and *saakhar* in Russian. The Latin term *succarum* is an Arabic derivation, reflected in the French term *sucre* and the English *sugar*. But *shakkar* had a twin travelling companion called *khand* — a word shared by Sanskrit, Tamil and Punjabi for cooked sugar. *Khand* was also adopted in Persia and travelled with the Arabs who re-assimilated the delicate flavours of Persian cuisine and took the 'sweet' culture to new heights of delicacies: preserved fruits coated in sugar, fruit jellies, almond and pistachio sweets, *baklava* and *halva*, marzipan and stuffed dates. Turkey adapted its local cuisine to sugar and borrowed from Persia and the Arab world to produce a range of sweets with delightful names like the *nightingale's nest*, *twisted turban*, *lady's lips*, *lady's navel* and even one called the *vizir's finger*!

Let us also follow the journeys of the word *khanda*. In Persian and Arabic it became *qand* and *shakkar qandi*. It was then assimilated in the areas under Arab rule: *zucchero candi* in Italian (Sicily's great indebtedness to those influences includes *cassata*); *azucar cande* in Spanish; and subsequently *assùcar candi* in Portuguese, *sucre candi* in French and on to *sugar candy* and *candy* in English.

The Abbasid Dynasty, Caliphs of Baghdad, who ruled the Arab Empire from AD 750 to 1258, gave much of the impetus for the sweetening of the near East and parts of Europe. They introduced sugarcane cultivation throughout the region west of Baghdad: Syria, Cyprus, Sicily, Southern Spain, Egypt and Morocco.

Then came the return flight of the boomerang. Ibn Batutta, while travelling through Upper Egypt in 1336, was amazed at the number of sugar processing factories he encountered. He came across eleven sugar factories in the town of Mallawi alone. In the middle ages, Egypt became famous for producing refined crystallised sugar, which was being imported into India. How we relish some *saunf* (anise) and *mishree* as a digestive after our meals. *Mishree* — from *mishr* — Egypt.

But hold on, there is more. We have yet another word for sugar in India, one that is associated with a country east of our subcontinent — *cheenee*. Strange and intriguing, for we don't normally associate anything sweet with Chinese cuisine. However, China began importing sugar from India in the first millennium BC. In time the Chinese started cultivating it and learnt sugar processing methods both from the Indians and the Egyptians. By the 18th century China had become one of the leading exporters of refined sugar from its plantations in Guandong province and Taiwan, rivalling the European colonial plantations in the Caribbean.

But the global voyage of sugar was not without its share of some bitter-sweet tragedy. Europe acquired its passion for sweets even though sugar was considered an item of luxury well into the 18th century. Only the affluent could afford it. It was not long before the Europeans got so addicted to sugar that Britain alone 'required' over 17 million African slaves and thousands of Indian indentured labour in their Caribbean colonies to produce this 'white gold', as they termed it. Sugar production was to become so lucrative that while millions perished in the plantations, the companies benefited enormously from the profits. They invested the overflowing coffers into Britain's machines that fuelled the Industrial Revolution — turning dreams into reality for some and nightmares into reality for others.

10

Tongue Untied

My husband's parents lived a long and happy life together. My father-in- law died at the age of 94 and my mother-in-law is still alive. However, once a day in all their years of wedded life they engaged in a battle in which neither won. Every afternoon at lunch my mother-in-law would declare: '*dahi baut mitthi hai*' (The yogurt is very sweet).

My father-in-law would gently correct her: '*Mitthi nahin, dahi mittha hai*'. For my mother-in-law yogurt was feminine, but her husband maintained it was masculine! One Punjabi family was from Dera Ismail Khan, the other from Doaba. They would keep arguing till the meal came to an end. And this carried on every day for at least 60 years of their married life. Now who was correct? Thank goodness neither of them was formulating language policies! Otherwise the one with the loudest voice would have won and imposed his or her language, and turned the other into a dialect as happened in so many places.

In the late 17th century an assertive Parisian aristocracy declared the Parisian tongue as the national language even though half the French population did not speak it at all and only 12–13 per cent spoke it correctly. The less assertive ones were forced to accept the label 'dialect' for their mother tongue. Italy's multilingual societies fared no better. At the time of Italy's unification in 1860, only 2.5 per cent of the population spoke the branch of Italian that was imposed on them. Multilingual societies were viewed as underdeveloped. Strangely it was felt that assimilation of all the peoples and all the languages into a single homogenised whole was progress. Linguists were assigned the tricky task of finding 'suitable scientific justifications' to support the political agenda. Language was approached as something lifeless, static and a conglomeration of dead signs, which needed to be channelled and directed. There were, it transpired, ostensibly rational languages and irrational ones, developed ones and underdeveloped ones — all linked to human development. In those times the wise ones had declared that languages spoken by numerically smaller peoples would inevitably die out along with the people, and cited the Czechs and Basques as examples. It has proven otherwise and the Czechs and the Basques continue to flourish.

Many governments around the world followed these European policies on national languages, belittling and designating the vast majority of languages as dialects subservient to the imposed national language.

History has shown that much of what we took at at face value is questionable. Perhaps we should do away with the term dialect altogether and find a nobler term. More so as the linguists themselves are in disagreement as to what differentiates a language from a dialect. We are told that the number of languages varies between 2,700 and 3,000. Is that plausible, given that just the Native American languages add up to 2000?

Each language is unique with its own long history, always in a state of flux. And each has evolved in different ways depending on the locale and the peoples' needs. But none has ever existed in pristine isolation.

Take the Saami, who live in the northern regions of Russia's Cola peninsula, Finland, Sweden and Norway. They are reindeer breeders and move with their herds across thousands of kilometres in summer. Nils Eira, a Saami, looks after a herd of 2,000 reindeer, and knows 1,200 words for reindeer: 'We classify them by age, sex, colour, antlers'. The Saamis too were considered the 'doomed' people, and were denied education in their mother tongue. Fortunately that is no longer the case.

The Mongols, famed horse breeders, distinguish 300 colours for horses. Languages of the peoples of the far north, including the Eskimos, are agglutinative, i.e. words are formed by combining roots and affixes. Some languages have four roots just for 'snow' and, consequently, countless number of words for snow!

The Daghestanis narrate a legend about the time when God's messenger, the distributor of languages, arrived in Daghestan. He got caught in a snowstorm and, rather than climb the steep cliffs of the region and visit every populated area, he chose to scatter his burden of the remaining 30-odd languages to the winds. Next morning the Daghestanis woke up to discover that they could not understand one another and to this day, single-language villages exist in the region.

In the early days of Perestroika the Lithuanian writer Yestimas Martsinkyavichyus, pleaded for his language with the words

> The earth which we have inherited from our ancestors is our earth. We call it Lithuania and do not want this name to disappear either from the geographical map or from the languages of different peoples. …The language which we speak and which we are proud of — is our language. It does not want to threaten anyone nor does it turn down anyone. Just like other languages it wants to live.

�֍

11

The Kashmiri Magician

◙

One of the more popular folktales which is shared across Central Asia is about a Kashmiri magician who can turn himself into anything he wants — a bird, a flower and even a horse. One day a poor farmer's son is brought to him to study magic. However, the magician, a nasty old man, refuses to teach the boy anything. Instead he throws him into a cellar, forcing him to do menial work. It is his daughter who secretly teaches the boy all the intricacies of magic. In time the boy falls in love with the *Badshah's* daughter and determines to marry her. The poor boy, rich girl story is logically embellished with a father figure who places numerous hurdles in the boy's path that he has to overcome in order to marry. Meanwhile, the old Kashmiri discovers that his daughter has passed on his skills to the boy. Enraged, he pursues the boy. The boy turns into a horse, so the Kashmiri turns into an eagle. The transformations go on till the boy finally outwits the Kashmiri to marry the girl.

I found copies of this folktale, richly illustrated for children, in Samarkand. Later I discovered it in a collection of Uzbek fairy tales. I was drawn, naturally, to the Kashmiri, and the fact that he was a magician. How come he was not a local *shaman* or an Uzbek? And why was he an anti-hero?

Like all other folktales this too is multi-layered. We need to peel away layer after layer to unravel some of its connections. Kashmir, since ancient times, was a region of Tantric practices. Tantra, derived from the Sanskrit root *tan*, means to expand. It's teaching advocates proactive engagement with the world and offers ways and means for the human being to expand his consciousness to the fullest. Tantrics maintain that it is possible to attain *nirvana* or enlightenment in one lifetime, but in order to do so, one has to undergo extremely rigorous practices to multiply one's mental and physical powers. Magic is inseparable from Tantra, whose practices arouse the dormant psychic energies of the body. Not surprisingly, Marco Polo, the 13th century traveller, mentions the 'magicians' of Kashmir:

> They are adepts beyond all others in the art of magic; insomuch that they can compel their idols, although by nature dumb and deaf, to speak. They can likewise obscure the day, and perform many other miracles.

Tantra teachings and practices were subsequently absorbed into Buddhism. The great Tantric, Padmasambhava, who spread Buddhism in Tibet, was from the Swat valley, another Tantric stronghold. It is quite likely that Tantric Buddhism travelled from Kashmir and Swat to Afghanistan, the Pamirs, Soghdiana (Samarkand and its environs), and eastwards towards China. Archaeologists have found numerous Tantric images in the Pamir and Afrasiab areas. Moreover, Kashmir and Ladakh were also on the trade route to Central Asia and beyond, and served the innumerable traders from Peshawar, Multan and Kashmir.

This could explain the presence of a Kashmiri Tantric (who may well have been a Buddhist) in the folktale. With the passage of time Buddhism went into oblivion and was replaced by Sufism and Islam. The Kashmiri became simply a magician (*jadoogar*), without any association with Buddhist Tantric powers (*jogi*). More centuries elapsed. By the mid 19th century the Russians were beginning to control parts of Central Asia. Initially it was mandatory for Russian officers stationed in Central Asia to speak Hindustani/Urdu, the lingua franca of the region because of the presence of a large number of traders from the Indian subcontinent. Once Central Asia was conquered, Russia wanted its own credit banks to control the money-lending in these regions. They had to get the local population out of the 'clutches', as they termed it, of the Indian money-lenders. A vilification campaign was successfully carried out and the Indian merchants were gradually driven out of the region. That would explain the next transform-ation in the folktale when the Kashmiri was turned into the antagonist of the boy hero. But the story would have been dull or incomplete without the element of magic. My guess is that at this point in time the daughter enters the plot to play the role of the teacher. Who knows, in due course, if the links between Kashmir and Central Asia remain weak, the antagonist will no longer remain a Kashmiri.

Such transformations occur in all folktales and in all societies be-cause certain elements lose their historical or cultural relevance and are replaced by others. In European fairy tales, for instance, Christianity's campaign against paganism resulted in the trans-formation of local healers into witches brewing some horrid brew. Alternately, if folktales arrive from another country, they are modified to suit the culture of the receiving community, as was the case of the *Panchatantra* tales which travelled across the globe.

12

Encounters

▣

We certainly are living on a shrunken planet, inundated with images, news and data from across the world through the media and internet. Despite that, travelling to another country can still produce confusion and mystification, not only for the traveller, but also for the local residents.

A Bashkir family friend with a delectable name, Aisloo (beautiful moon), arrived from Moscow with a shopping list which included a saree request — a silk saree with cucumbers all over it.

'*Yes, my friend saw an Indian lady in Moscow wearing a saree with cucumbers and simply fell in love with it*', Aisloo smiled smugly.

It was an impossible request! Not even in our wildest imagination could we regard cucumbers as something aesthetically pleasing to the eye. We tried to dissuade Aisloo but to no avail. At the shop I lowered my voice and hesitantly asked the saleswoman to show us sarees with cucumbers. Her reaction, thank goodness, was the same as ours — disbelief. Moments later there was an excited squeal from the other end of the shop followed by a triumphant Aisloo marching towards us with three sarees in her arms — all with so-called cucumber motifs…

'*Aisloo!*' I said, '*these are ambees, mangoes, not cucumbers! Surely you've seen this popular motif on Bashkir, Iranian and Central Asian carpets? Haven't you heard of badaami from the word badaam (almonds)? That's what this design motif is called in all these regions.*'

But Aisloo, having lived away from home for so long, remained blissfully unaware. It was the cucumber that came closest to her identifiable cultural image and she returned home happily with her cucumber silk saree.

Aisloo may have got the decorative motifs wrong but what about others who are shocked by our public behaviour? How many Europeans and Americans on their first visit to the Indian subcontinent are appalled by the callousness and 'public indifference' to the multitudes of tuberculosis patients throwing up blood on the streets till someone explains to them the pleasures of eating *paan*.

These two incidents are instructive and reveal that every time a cross-cultural encounter takes place, one culture poses unpredictable questions to the Other. And every time these questions are asked, each culture begins to question itself about characteristics that it had simply taken for granted.

Take the case of a visiting Soviet professor at the Russian Centre in the university. She came out of her first lecture very agitated. It had taken her one-and-a-half hours to repeatedly attempt to explain in Russian some very simple concept to the students. According to her, whenever she asked the students whether they had understood, they simply shook their heads. This upset her so much that she was ready to pack her bags. Somewhat puzzled, a colleague finally asked her whether the students had shaken their heads in a sort of sideways manner.

'*Yes! Yes!*' she exclaimed.

'*Well, that is how many of us indicate "yes".*'

It takes time for foreigners coming to our country to mentally adjust to this alien gesture which is neither one of negation nor affirmation.

Fritz Staal, a 70-year-old Dutch scholar of Sanskrit, recounted his first day as a student in Madras University. After the lecture by a renowned Sanskrit scholar, a student asked Fritz whether he had enjoyed it.

'*I'm afraid, I do not speak Tamil*', Fritz replied.

'*What Tamil? The lecture was in English*'.

Today Professor Staal speaks Tamilian English fluently.

Then there was a lady from Siberia married to an Indian. She recounted to her mother how in India guests were greeted with a glass of water.

'*Water! Is that hospitality?*' was her mother's horrified response.

This was an understandable response from somebody residing in the sub-zero temperatures of Siberia where water is never really drunk on its own. But, by the same logic, the hot Indian climate influences our sense of hospitality. A person entering a house from the sweltering heat is always greeted with that mandatory glass of water with other refreshments to follow. How easy it is to misinterpret unfamiliar cultural traits and turn them into derogatory characteristics.

But there seems to be no limit to the foreigners' sense of bewilderment, be it our gestures, habits or even clothes. Another of our family gems is about the Chinese laundry man who stood outside the door of an Indian student's flat in New York. The student's father, on a visit to his daughter, liked to wear a smart *achkan* and white, starched *chooridaar pyjamas*, which were regularly dispatched to the laundry. The Chinese stood there with an apologetic expression on his face, shuffled his feet and finally threw his arms wide apart and blurted out, '*I'm sorry to disturb you but can I please see the gentleman who has this enormous girth and extremely long and thin legs?*'

❈

13

Head to Toe

回

In Afghanistan a turban is called a *lungi.* What happened? Did it slide down to the hips on its journey southwards to the Punjab where the *lungi* is the wrap around the waist? Imagine the hilarious mix-ups arising in a conversation between a raucous Punjabi and a hot-blooded Afghan centred around the *lungi!* Fortunately in Peshawar, a town inhabited by both Afghar.s and Punjabis, a way out was found to avoid misunderstanding. To distinguish the waist *lungi* from the turban *lungi,* the former was termed *majhi* or middle *lungi.*

Indeed, a certain type of *majhi lungi* in Peshawar was called a *mashaddi lungi.* To understand why, we would need to journey to the shores of the Caspian Sea where Mashad, a town in Persia's Khorasan district, traditionally wove a grey coloured cotton fabric. At some point of time, according to my Bherochi father, a number of weavers from Mashad settled down in Bhera and continued weaving the *mashaddi lungis.*

Other voyagers fared better on their southward travels. *Deva* — the Persian term for demon, got elevated to the rank of a deity by the time it reached India. An intimidating word like *shaitan* (Satan) was transformed into a rather endearing term. In North Indian languages — this word is also associated with children, implying mischievous and naughty, with none of its negative overtones. Journeys can also bring about a gender change. An Iranian lady was taken aback by Indian images of the sun and the moon sporting a moustache. In Persia they are both feminine.

How did a wonderful Persian word for 'rose water', *jalaab*, take on a rather unpleasant association with an upset stomach in Punjabi? Was it a prankster to whom we owe the new meaning.?

There are numerous migratory words associated with geographical areas (remember the turkey bird's travels). An obsolete name for pearls in Russian was *bisera* — a likely derivative of the port of Basra, famous for exporting pearls. Similarly, the earlier Russian word for indigo was linked to Lahore. Known in Afghanistan and Persia as *lahori,* this dye became *lavra* (pronounced *lavraa*) by the time it entered the Russian language. It is mentioned in an account book of the Russian State Treasury of 1705: *'the dye Lavrá from India was sold in Moscow for 17,568 roubles'.* The Indian word for indigo, *neel,* is also found in the Persian, Turkic and Arabic languages, and got transformed in Georgian into *lila.* The Portuguese word for indigo, *aneel* (or anile), and the French word, l'anil, is derived from the Arabic, *al-neel.* Aniline is from the root *anil* , but the term now refers generally to chemical-based dyes.

It is anybody's guess how and why the expression 'checkmate' (from the Persian, *shah maat* or 'the king is dead') became the Russian term for chess, *shakhmati.* All one can say is that it proved rather prophetic and lucky for the future world champions.

Although I have taken up some word transformations through journeys, even within a language of a given culture the meanings of words are in a constant state of flux. There was a time when the English word 'nice' meant stupid and ignorant; and penis in Latin meant a tail. But it is not as if this flux existed only in the past. Today we are constant witnesses to all sorts of fascinating adaptations and ingenuities. In America, a lady who was habitually lucky in finding parking spaces claimed that she had the 'parking karma'! Closer to home, I overheard a car driver refusing to drive along a particular route because it had 'house full', meaning traffic jam, on that road. He also used the same phrase to describe a river in flood. These new adaptations of words, used freely in local Indian languages, add novel dimensions to conventional connotations. At times these words and phrases retain barely tenuous connections with the original English ones. Another popular phrase, 'couple cases', is used by hoteliers to describe the booking category of newly-wedded couples on their honeymoon. Then there are 'time pass', 'adjust' and 'goft' (abbreviated from 'government'). A friend of ours was touring the Chamba valley in the Himalayas and stopped at a small wayside temple. She asked a local passerby about the temple and to whom it was dedicated.

'*Woh to ji Hidamba devi ka mandir hai, jo Bheem ji kee misses thee…*' Although the subtle nuances get lost in the Latin script, I shall attempt a translation: 'It is Hidamba devi's temple, the one who was Bheem ji's Mrs.'

(Bheem was one of the Pandava brothers in the *Mahabharata*). I wonder if some of our self-appointed language purists will object to the renaming of all the female consorts of the Indian pantheon as Mrs. Deities in heaven.

14

Home and Away

▣

Borders are imaginary lines drawn by rulers who want to impart permanence to their whims. These lines divide families living on either side of a river or they divide linguistic groups (the Punjabis, Kashmiris and Bengalis). While politicians and the military debate and argue over borders, there is another deeper reality that defies these divides.

Over 22 years ago a large contingent of Pakistani painters attended the Delhi Triennale. Some of them taught at the Lahore College of Art, others were from Karachi. The group included the painter Zahoor-ul-Akhlaq and his ceramist wife Sheherazad. At one of the receptions, the conversation turned to pre-Partition times. One Pakistani painter was nostalgic about Delhi's Lodhi Gardens where she was regularly taken as a child, another recalled the Civil Lines area. Many of the guests, it transpired, were born on our side of the border, and the majority of Punjabi *Delhiwalas* were from what is today Pakistan. A couple of Indians wanted to know about Anarkali bazaar. They were told that although Lahore is the same old town as it was in earlier times, Anarkali has changed beyond recognition. The guests could not understand why every visiting Indian insisted on being taken to Anarkali. It seemed as though parents, grandparents, relatives and even friends of relatives had forced a promise out of the poor traveller to visit this bazaar and return with a detailed description to fill the gaps in their fuzzy, fading but fond memories. From Anarkali the conversation once again reverted to memories of home. My husband, who was born in Murree, had a vivid recollection of his maternal grandfather's house in Lahore where he grew up. There was a huge garden at the back of the house which had a circular entrance. He seemed to recall a canal nearby. Somebody suggested it might be the Canal Road, another wondered if it could be the Upper Mall. My husband seemed at a loss initially but eventually decided that Upper Mall did indeed ring a bell.

Sheherazad, who had been silent all this while, suddenly asked, '*Do you remember the number of your house?*'

'*No, but I can ask my mother*'. With these words he disappeared only to reappear a few moments later, '*Number 90, Upper Mall*'.

There was a split-second silence and then Zahoor exclaimed, '*That's the number of <u>our</u> house! And it does have a circular entrance.*'

'*What about a black and white stone pattern on the entrance floor?*'

'*Yes, yes, that's also there*'. Sheherazad added, '*The moment you mentioned the entrance I guessed it must be the same place. That house was allotted to my father — a refugee after the Partition.*'

This indeed was magical realism. Out of the millions of possibilities some inexplicable energy had brought us together.

'*That house*', my husband explained, '*was built by my grandfather who was Chief Engineer Canals. He constructed a bungalow colony and it was named after him: Bawa Park.*'

'*It's still Bawa Park*', came the Lahori response.

Over time Zahoor and his wife became our friends. On our first trip to Lahore we visited their home — known as 1 Bawa Park. My husband relived his childhood memories by going from room to room with the rest of us following him.

But that was not the end of the story. Years later our son went to study in England. Amongst his numerous friends were, of course, Pakistanis. It was a repeat of both our university years abroad. We too had had lots of Pakistani friends — a natural Punjabi affinity perhaps, borders notwithstanding. So when my father occasionally bemoaned the severed ties between the two countries I would tell him of my son's experience. He belongs to the second post-Partition generation, yet many of his closest friends are Lahoris, one of whom gave him his first cooking lesson. Farooq, aptly nicknamed Mamta, regularly fed the semi-starved and penniless students in the London hostel. It was in Mamta's *'langar'* that Martand met Rafay. They immediately hit it off as they both shared an interest in music and witticisms.

This is the story we were told. Soon after their first meeting our son casually walked into Rafay's room. As Rafay was busy at his desk, Martand approached the pin-board and started looking at the photographs. Suddenly he let out a yell.

'Hey, what's my grandmother's house doing on your board?'

'That's my home', Rafay replied nonplussed.

'Shut up! Next you'll be telling me that you are related to that painter Zahoor', my son retorted.

'But I am…'

And so it transpired that Rafay, my son's close friend, turned out to be Zahoor and Sheherazad's nephew and had grown up in the same house — the house of my husband's childhood.

✳

15

Wear with All

◻

The doorman at the Intercontinental Hotel in Phnom Penh is dressed in a Kaiser helmet, a short white military jacket with gold buttons, a silk sarong and polished black boots over long white socks. The royal dress of the King of Nepal's was an English jacket worn over his *kurta* and *chooridaar pyjamas*. A common sight amongst Delhi's early morning walkers are women in long nightgowns with a *dupatta* casually thrown over their shoulders. These are just a few examples of 'mix and match' wear [**Plate 8**].

Yet in parts of the world, governments and ultra nationalists are busy forcing dress codes on soft targets, especially womens' attire, trying to invent some ephemeral 'authenticity' and 'identity'. Recently, the 'secular' French government banned wearing headscarves to work and school, contending that only French identity could be expressed. Are tattoos, nose rings, belly buttons and *salwaars* part of the French identity? The ban on headscarves snowballed to Belgium, Germany, the UK, Italy and the Netherlands. Thousands of miles away some Indian Muslim clerics launched a campaign against Sania Mirza's tennis outfits. The right-wing Bharatiya Janta Party does not lag behind in this crusade. Let us join them on their journey in search of 'roots'.

Not so long ago the youth wing of the BJP, the ABVP, came out with a directive about an acceptable dress code for women in Kanpur. Their concern was truly laudable since our ancient scriptures state that the gods dwell only where women are respected. These tight-fitting jeans worn by our girls, if nothing else, are so unsuitable for our climate.

But what else can our girls wear? The *salwaar kameez* is out. It has been implanted on the subcontinent by Turks from Central Asia whose women and men galloped about freely on horses. What a comfortable dress for horseback and motorbike rides! This dress has overtaken our entire country, so much so that the *salwaar kameez* is associated today with this subcontinent rather than with the Turkic peoples of Central Asia. We proudly declare that princess Diana and Cherie Blair wore these designer outfits. Accepting the *salwaar* seems out of the question.

Should all our women then go back to wearing the beautiful, graceful *saree* (assuming no other dress existed earlier)? But which *saree* and of which geographical area should serve as the model? That is not an easy choice. The popular *saree* worn in Indian cities today was an invention of Rabindranath Tagore's sister-in-law, Gyanodanandini Tagore, who wanted to attend the British *Durbar* in suitable attire and created a blend of the European gown with the local *saree* . In the book series, *Sarees of India*, it is stated that in three Indian states alone, there are 25 different ways of tying a saree (ten in Madhya Pradesh, ten in Bihar, five in Bengal). Moreover, the lengths, widths, patterns and fabric differ from village to village.

But before researching the *saree*, it might be necessary to rouse the public into organising huge bonfires for all foreign apparel, like in Gandhi ji's time. Next, women would have to take a vow of going *swadeshi* and shunning everything foreign. Then with a cry of Vande Mataram, jeans, dresses, *salwaar kameezes, saree* blouses and petticoats would be hurled into the bonfire. Blouses and petticoats was no slip of the pen. This tight-fitting, and climatically unsuitable attire was also forced upon us by the British colonialists. Remember the riots in Calcutta and Kerala in the 19th century when people resisted this imposition? Ever since then the Indian woman has suffered the heat stoically and in silence. Undoubtedly the 21st century will liberate them from all foreign pollutants, thanks to the ABVP storm-troopers.

While the woman drapes herself in a long unstitched garment, what about the men? Are they going to attend corporate meetings dressed in badly stitched trousers? Is it not time for the Sangh

Parivaar, or the ABVP, to pay attention to the Indian mens' dress code, including the *khaki* shorts of their RSS brigades? For it has been aptly stated that 'he does not preach what he has not practiced till he has practiced what he preaches'. So what should our men wear? A handspun *dhoti* with a wraparound shawl? Some of our ancient advocates were indeed against stitched clothing. In the meantime perhaps one of their brighter students could be given the task of researching the topic, 'The Origins of Khaki Shorts in Vedic Texts'.

But there is cheer in the air and space for reason for Amartya Sen has explained the other side of the forced identity campaign: 'The individual belongs to many different groups and it is up to him or her to decide which of those groups he or she would like to give priority.'

16

I Am Bandit

On the Thai island of Koh Samui there is a speedboat with a rather strange name, 'I am Bandit'. Could it be a warning about the reckless speed of the man at the wheel or is the man boasting about his 'profession', or else, could it just be a way of warding off the evil eye? I decided it must be the latter. The Thais are amongst the gentlest of people who are forever smiling. I never witnessed any quarrels on the streets, or any impatient honking of cars. Even the demonstrations in Bangkok against Prime Minister Thaksin were orderly and peaceful — truly a *Suvarnabhoom*i (land of gold in Sanskrit), so aptly named by Emperor Ashoka in the 2nd or 3rd century BC. Yet every morning and evening 'I am Bandit' hurtled at break-neck speed, upsetting the tranquil turquoise waters as it headed towards the distant jetty where it disgorged its petrified passengers.

At the end of two weeks I had collected a few familiar sounding words. I became aware that during the period of ancient contacts with our subcontinent, Sanskrit terms had been introduced to the Thai language through Khmer. With this list I headed for a shop where luckily the owner spoke English. I discovered that '*sok*' (happiness) was indeed from '*sukh*' and *singha* was lion. However, Thai is a tonal language with five different pitches that requires one to 'sing' the word exactly at the right pitch otherwise the Thais might just get it all wrong. Imagine, a simple word like '*mai*' can mean 'wood', 'silk', 'burn', 'new' or 'not', all depending on the tone and pitch of one's pronunciation. I had had a very frustrating morning trying to get soap in the hotel. Whichever way I sang the word I still got a blank expression in return. It was my acting prowess that got me what I desperately needed. We must all seem tone deaf to the Thais who have given up on foreigners incapable of pronouncing their names correctly, and so have found easy equivalents. There is Ping Pong, an energetic young girl running a resort and two sisters, Tip and Top, maintaining a plant nursery. But still,

'*Why would somebody call their boat "bandit"?*' I asked,

The Thai lady seemed surprised by my question.

'*Oh-oh-ooo, bandit is a good word. Means wise person*'.

Only then did something click in my brain and I saw the connection between 'bandit' and '*pandit*'. Yes of course, the voiceless consonant 'p' (in *pandit)* was replaced by a voiced '*b*'. A similar change occurred with the word *mantri* (minister), which became '*mandarin*' in Chinese. Then again, I don't envy our ex-minister of Human Resource Development, Pandit Murli Manohar Joshi being hosted by the Thais!

These two words are relatively simple examples of phonetic adjustments that are easy to decipher. I decided to find out a little more about the Khmer language which, unlike Thai, is not tonal.

In the Angkor period of Cambodian history (9th–15th century), numerous Sanskrit and Pali words (by way of Buddhism) were absorbed into the Khmer language, and subsequently into Thai, since Thailand was a Khmer colony. The new words adjusted to their new homes, imbibing the rules of pronunciation and sounds of the local languages. The voiced consonants in the numerous Sanskrit and Pali words, though written accurately, became voiceless in speech. The Khmer equivalent of Garuda is pronounced *Krut*, Brahma is written *Preah Brum* but pronounced *Prom*, and the incense *dhoop* becomes *thoop*. The reverse too can happen, i.e. when voiceless consonants become voiced: *tara* (star) is pronounced *dara* and the deity Varuna is Phirun.

Once we become aware of this it should not be too difficult to trace back to the Sanskrit or Pali originals. Nothing can be further from the truth. Take Angkor Wat, the magnificent 12th century temple dedicated to Vishnu in Cambodia. The first word Angkor is derived from the word for town, '*nagar*'. The initial sound 'n' changed its place with 'a' and 'nag' became 'angk', ending with 'or' instead of 'ar'. All this is about phonetic adaptation into a host language.

Does the following passage make sense?

'*Preah Ream, Neang Seda and Preah Leak continued on again, meeting a yeak…*'

This Khmer or Cambodian text of the Ramayana translates as, 'Rama, Sita and Laxman continued on again, meeting a demon …'

One needs expert guidance to comprehend how *gaja* (elephant in Sanskrit) becomes *khot*, or *vajra* (diamond) turns into *pet*! But the choicest examples of phonetic transference into the Khmer language I am leaving for the readers to guess: the first one is not too difficult. The equivalent word for India is *bpra — dtayh-eun — dee-a*; Buddha is *Bpray — ah bpoot*; and Buddhism logically follows as *Bpoot-ta — saa — s'naa*. Please try singing them in their Thai variant to get a more authentic sound.

17

Badghizi

◫

He repeated his question for the fourth time, '*What do you think of this carpet?*'

The first three times the Italian's questions had been answered with a plate of melons, followed by peaches, and finally *kishmish* and tea. This time Badghizi merely smiled. His smile also seemed to be the signal for another large dish of *pullao* to appear miraculously. It was typical, should I say, of Afghan or Turkmen or Central Asian hospitality.

Badghizi, sensing the edge in the Italian's tone, decided to break his silence.

'*Please try these Samarkandi peaches. After lunch I need time to talk to the carpet. Find out from her her age, her life…*'

Seeing the look of contempt on Stefano's face, Badghizi paused. It was the silence of a sage.

'*Yes*', he continued, '*The carpet will tell me if one person's hands wove it or if there were many hands involved; whether it was woven for a special occasion or for day to day use; whether it belongs to one clan or whether others entered its folds…*'

'What do you mean — different clans?'

'*Supposing a girl from the Saryk clan marries a Bashiri boy then the girl could introduce some Bashiri motifs into her Saryk design next time she weaves a carpet. Anyway, I have to also ask the carpet the number of knots she has, whether she is made of silk or wool or both; whether natural dyes have been used or chemical ones.…. All this takes time. Please eat*'.

The object of discussion, in the meantime, lay in a corner of a vast hall overflowing with carpets. Some were spread out one on top of another, while others were rolled up. We too were perched on a pile of carpets. This hall was at the furthest end of a carpet factory in Samarkand. And Badghizi is part of its history.

I first met Badghizi in 1986 in Soviet-occupied Kabul where his family was trading in carpets. His daughters and wife wove the carpets while the men looked after the business. It was in Kabul that I stepped into the fascinating world of carpets. Till then I had no idea that the art of Turkic carpet weaving dates back at least 2,500 years. The carpet weaving culture of the sheep breeders includes enormous carpets and small tent bags, salt bags, camel covers and door *purdahs*, each of them a work of art. I learnt that the Baluch carpets are woven by the Afghans, whereas the *Saryk, Mauri* and *Bashiri* by the Turkmen. Traditionally the name of the carpet is determined by its central geometric medallion or *gul* (flower), which identifies the clan. For instance, the *Saryk* carpet with its central *Saryk gul* is woven by the women of the Saryk clan. My introduction to carpets was consequential to my research about the Central Asian peoples of the Soviet Union and how they had settled in Afghanistan. Badghizi's family had fled from Turkmenistan in the 1930s at the time of forced collectivisation in the USSR. They managed to survive and piece together their existence as migrants, keeping alive their carpet weaving tradition. In the meantime, as the USSR industrialised, machines began replacing hand-woven carpets, and chemical dyes were substituting natural dyes.

Some more years passed. Just before our departure for Samarkand where my husband and I were engaged in a UNESCO project, I was requested to carry indigo for Mr Badghizi in Samarkand. Could it be our Badghizi? We were delighted to meet a long-lost friend and asked him what had brought him to Samarkand. This was his story.

The political situation deteriorated during the Taliban regime, forcing Badghizi to once again pack his bags and leave Kabul. Some family members moved to Delhi. Badghizi, with his two daughters, came to Uzbekistan — a new country also in the throes of great turmoil. The old man realised that there was widespread unemployment and many people had lost their carpet weaving skills. He approached the Uzbek government for permission to set up a carpet training workshop in an abandoned factory. Within two years Badghizi and his family had trained 200 girls in carpet weaving. At the end of her training, each girl was presented a loom to take home and earn a livelihood. Badghizi reintroduced natural dyes. The indigo I had brought was meant as proof for the sceptics who attended his carpet weaving workshops, and who had forgotten about the existence of original natural dyes that went into the making of these fabulous carpets.

I do not know where Badghizi is today. Has his scattered family re-united? I wonder if he returned to Kabul. All I can say is that life's enormous upheavals and countless displacements did not make him bitter or cynical. Instead he simply continued to spread his goodness and knowledge through his art, wherever he went.

18

Blackouts

New history textbooks for Indian schools are now available — an effort to neutralise the communal BJP's interventions into school education made during their years in power. And 'argumentative Indians' are already discussing their pros and cons. History, at any rate, is written or rewritten to suit a particular ideology, so one naturally wonders whether there is an objective history at all.

In 2005, one of the contenders for the Pope's throne was Cardinal Francis Arinze of Nigeria. Objections were raised in the Western press and Arinze admitted that Europe was not ready for a black Pope. I am certain that the majority of Europeans were genuinely kept in the dark about the history of their own church. Full credit must be given to the Europeans because they rewrote their history in a more ingenious way than we have been able to do in our parts of the world. We tend to throw out whole chunks of historical time, which then vanish into black holes. The subtlety with which rewriting was done in parts of Europe is illuminating. For instance, some important historical characters were renamed and their real places of origin obscured by Roman place names so that they could be absorbed into national histories. There seems a reluctance to accept that European history, like any other history, is a repository of the accumulated wisdom, ideas and achievements of diverse people from all over the world, including Africa.

Between the 2nd and the 5th centuries there were three African Popes: Saint Victor I (AD 189–199), Saint Miltiades (AD 311–314) and Saint Gelasius I (AD 492–496). Each of them made significant contributions to the Western church. Saint Victor I decreed celebrating Easter on a Sunday, while Saint Gelasius finalised the list of books that compose the Bible.

There were other seminal contributions to the Western church by African theologians, some of whom are acknowledged as the early Christian Fathers. The choice of Latin rather than Greek as the liturgical language of the Roman Catholic church and the formulation of the concept of Trinity was introduced by a Tunisian named Tertullian (2nd–3rd century AD). He lived in Carthage (now in Tunisia) and is regarded as the 'Father of the Western Church'. Wilken in *The Encyclopedia Britannica* says about him:

> As the initiator of ecclesiastical Latin, he was instrumental in shaping the vocabulary and thought of Western Christianity for the next 1,000 years.

Another Father, Origen (182–251), a prolific writer and a contemporary of Tertullian, was Egyptian. He is also considered the Father of Theology and of the early Christian church. The concept of Original Sin and the Immaculate Conception (much in the news for the controversy surrounding *The Da Vinci Code* novel and film) was initiated by Saint Augustine (AD 354–430), an Algerian. He was born and brought up in the Algerian coastal town of Tagaste, now Souk-Ahras. Thus with all these non-European Fathers of their church, Europeans should have no problem accepting the recent genetic findings that trace the origin of all human ancestry to the African Eve — mother of all human races, including theirs.

While imagining the events of the Roman Empire, one should first erase the Hollywood images that are etched in our memories, because in the Roman Empire, white and non-white people mingled freely and blacks became Roman Emperors, military commanders, slaves as well as poets. The famous Triumphal Arch of Severus at the Forum of Rome and the Caracalla Baths (a must for tourists) were built by Septimius Severus and his son Caracalla of the Severan dynasty which ruled the Roman Empire between AD 193 and 225. It commenced with the Libyan, Septimius Severus (AD 193–211) whose wife was a Syrian, to be followed by a mixture of Libyan, Syrian, Tunisian and a Moroccan. Emperor Elagabalus (218–222), for instance, was also the hereditary head priest of the Syrian sun god El Gabal, or Baal. He arranged a wedding ceremony between El Gabal and the moon Goddess Urania in order to merge the Roman pantheon and the Syrian god. The African features of Septimius Severus and his sons are clearly discernable in their busts that are on view at the National Roman Museum [**Plate 9**].

One thousand years of Rome's foundation was celebrated with great fanfare during the reign of another Syrian Roman Emperor, Philip the Arab (AD 244–249). The special coins minted to commemorate that event have become rare collectors' items. Many 4th century writers consider him as the first Christian Roman Emperor since he allowed Christians to practice their religion openly.

In accepting cross-national contributions, and while unfolding some hidden layers of rejected history, I am attempting to start a dialogue that blows away the illusions of exclusivity. This is the first of other 'blackouts' in European history that will be discussed in the following pages.

✳

19

Oh Bokhara!

◙

My husband and I were sitting in a tiny café in the old part of Bokhara, overlooking the historical Chor Su market. As we sipped green tea in those small bowls, we wondered why we were feeling so much at home. Was it perhaps something to do with the welcoming energy of the place? Was it possible that when we are in strange places, our inner self can sense layers of the history of the place without any rhyme or reason. Some places give us an acute sense of discomfort while others seem to embrace us. Neither of us believes in coincidences and sure enough, the response to our speculations materialised out of nowhere. He was an old man with a grey beard, dressed in a long quilted *chapan* coat, in short, a being from another age. He looked at us and said: *'Hindistan'.* It was more of a statement for he immediately turned and pointed in the direction of the dilapidated gateway of the old city wall, and said, *'The Indian merchants entered from there. For two weeks they had to camp outside the city walls — quarantine period. Then they were allowed in and they headed straight for the hamaam'*, and he pointed to an old *hamaam* close to the Chor Su. *'After bathing they went to their Indian Caravansarai, see there?'*

Time stood still. We were transported into another era, imagining the camels tied to the rusty iron loops still visible along the outside of the city wall; the diverse groups of merchants from all corners of the world babbling in their own tongues or greeting old friends. When we came out of our reverie, the old man had vanished. We retraced our steps to the Chor Su dome imagining the hustle and bustle around the Indian jewellers in one corner, and carpet dealers in another. We knew about Bokhara carpets, those deep maroon carpets with large geometric medallions. But now we learnt that Bokharans don't weave carpets. The town was, however, the great trading centre of carpets. That explains how the carpets originating from there became known as Bokhara carpets, just as 'hindi' turned into a generic term for all spices in this region.

We were beginning to enjoy being in a time warp and decided to continue our leisurely stroll through the old town with its narrow winding lanes leading to the Labbe Haus, a square at the end of a water body. Could it be that it was here that the residents gathered for the poetry contests and exchanged anecdotes and tales? Somebody may have recounted the tale of Sohni and Mahiwaal, a favourite Punjabi folktale. Izzat, the son of a rich trader from Bokhara, comes to Chenab where he falls in love with Sohni, a potter's daughter. Instead of returning with the trading caravan he disguises himself and takes up a job as an ordinary Indian *mahiwaal* (cowherd) in Sohni's house. Although she is married off to somebody else, they continue to meet. One day, when Sohni is on her way to Mahiwaal, she drowns. He too jumps into the river and drowns, uttering his dying words: 'I'm mixing the soil of Bokhara and Punjab and handing it over to the mighty spirit of love'. This is only one of numerous Punjabi folktales with characters from Central Asia.

Our wanderings led us to the only functioning madrasa, outside which some young students were lazing in the sun. In 1832, Bokhara had 60 madrasas, about 366 institutes of higher learning and over 11 major libraries. In 1863, the Hungarian traveller and polyglot Armenius Vambery was overwhelmed by the love for learning in Bokhara and Samarkand:

> One cannot but be amazed by the zeal and readiness of both rulers and ordinary working people to donate for the construction and provision of the colleges of Bokhara…

Renowned scientists, philosophers and poets were associated with these great centres of learning. Who knows, over a 1,000 years ago two students may have sat arguing outside their institute, not knowing that their work would revolutionise European science and mathematics. Abu Ali ibn-Sina (980–1037), known in the West as Avicenna (the author of Canon of Medicine), was born in Afshana, a village on the outskirts of Bokhara. The other boy could have been Al Beruni, whose real name was Mohammed ibn Ahmed al-Khorezmi, i.e. from Khorezm in present-day Uzbekistan. Others who studied in Bokhara were Omar Khayyam and Hazrat Khwaja Muinuddin Chishti (1135–1229), the founder of the Sufi order in Ajmer.

Bokhara turned into a metaphor of the sublime, of splendour and grandeur. No wonder the 14th century Persian poet Hafiz, in a love poem addressed to a beautiful Turkic girl from Shiraz, ex-claimed that for that one Indian (i.e. black) beauty spot on her cheek, he would offer her both Samarkand and Bokhara.

Egher an Turki Shirazi
Bedest ared dili mara,
Be khali hinduish bakhshem
Samarkand u Bokhara.

20

Fiddler on the Loose

◻

Legend has it that en route to the Russian Embassy in Vienna a man disappeared. His name was Gerasim Lebedev, a self-taught violinist and a member of a group of musicians attached to Count Razumovsky, the ambassador designate. Lebedev was no Count, for his father was an ordinary clergyman. After his disappearance Lebedev travelled around Europe eking out a living playing his violin. And then all of a sudden he joined an English military band that was being sent to India. This was in 1785. The ship docked in Madras, where Lebedev resided for a couple of years and then left for Bengal.

On arrival in Calcutta he immediately made friends with the local residents, one of whom requested Lebedev to teach him the violin. The Russian agreed on condition that the Bengali teach him his language. And so it came about that the Russian musician was taught Bengali, a smattering of Sanskrit, Indian mathematics and the calendar system, while he taught his teacher the violin. Lebedev lived in India for 12 long years, immersing himself in the life around him. Incidentally, he was the founder of India's first European-style proscenium theatre which opened in Calcutta. With some help he translated two English comedies into Bengali, and also composed the music. These plays were performed with actors of both sexes — very unusual at the time. The British Raj, not too pleased by the phenomenal success of his theatre, forced its closure. Lebedev was left penniless and driven out of the country.

On his return home he set up a Sanskrit Press in St Petersburg in 1805, the first of its kind in Europe. His book, *An Impartial*

Review of the East Indian Brahminical System of Sacred Rites and Customs, was the precursor of Russian writings about India and its people. However, for a long time scholars shrugged off Lebedev's work as being unscientific (but also, I suspect, for not confining itself to later Orientalist clichés).

The book on India is both touching and humorous. Lebedev's knowledge of India was derived from his Bengali contacts. Consequently, everything he wrote about India was through Bengali pronunciation, which emphasises the sound 'o'. *'They have a language called Shomshkrit, also called Deb Nakor, and Prankrito, and a god called Krishto'.* He attempted to explain terms which even today are difficult to translate; thus he describes *'kalpa',* a measure of time, as chaos, and *'atma'* or soul is misconstrued as atmosphere. Unable to make head or tail of the bewildering number of deities and faiths, Lebedev, like other European travellers and Orientalists, sought out Christian parallels. Indian polytheism was reduced to a simple, easily understandable, Christian monotheism and the Trinity. Furthermore, Indians, according to Lebedev, also believe in the concept of the Immaculate Conception. Once that was sorted out it became relatively simple to deduce that Durga or Kali (the most important deity in Bengal) was the Virgin Mary, and Krishto (Krishna) was Jesus. The Indian Trinity, according to Lebedev, included Krishto, Shiva and Brahma. About creation he writes that god created a husband and wife as the lords over everything, again reminiscent of Adam and Eve. *'He named the man father himself — Bromgo (Brahma) and the wife — Bishoka, and she bore Bromgo a hundred children'.* Lebedev was not alone in attempting to find parallels between his familiar Christian ethos and a new and unknown culture. Other Europeans were also determined to 'discover' the single religious Book, similar to the Bible, which India never possessed. Some foreigner must have been so persistent that an Indian, unable to communicate the diverse and often contrary belief systems, gave up, and referred him to the *Bhagavata Gita.* This is like taking a chapter from an epic poem, say the *Iliad,* and construing it as the equivalent of the Bible.

Back in Petersburg, Lebedev attempted to give a pictorial representation of the multi-armed goddess Durga for his book. We can only assume that the long return journey took its toll on his memory. The multiple arms emanate not from the shoulders but from the elbows. He must have recalled that the female deity held a musical instrument, but which one? After wracking his brains he finally made do with a violin! And why not? It had, after all, opened the doors of Bengali homes to him. There still remained one more empty hand. Perhaps out of sheer desperation Lebedev placed what seems like an upturned bottle in it [**Plate 10**]. How fortunate for him that he did not live in the 21st century. He would have been taken to court, as was the case with a company in the USA, that depicted Ganesh, the elephant god, with a beer mug in his hand.

21

The Game of the Name

回

Golbasto Momaren Evlame Gurdilo Shefin Mully Ully Gue was the almighty Emperor of the Lilliputs. He, along with four of his subjects, could fit in the palm of a hand, but not so his name. Jonathan Swift wrote his novel, *Gulliver's Travels,* in the 1720s. It satirised dwarfs who boast with pompous names — ideas that he took from the real world. Nobody seems to have paid much attention to Swift because a century later in 1889 an obituary appeared:

> On the 9th of October the King of Portugal, Louis Philippe Marie Ferdinand Pierre d'Alcantara Antoine Michel Rafael Gabriel Gonzaga Xavier Francois d' Assise Jean Jules Auguste Volfande de Braganza Bourbon, known among the sovereigns of Europe as Luis I…died. Yesterday he was buried.

Some upstart in our part of the world would undoubtedly have quipped that before the last of the names was read out at the king's funeral, he would have probably been reborn. These names were primarily linked to Christian saints and had social significance in Europe. The longer the list of names, the higher was the social standing of the recipient of this burden. Ordinary members of the Spanish aristocracy, for instance, were permitted eight names, the upper echelons of aristocracy could notch up 16, and as for royalty, there was no limit. Commoners were permitted to have only one name. Remnants of these long name banners of identity remain in today's world. Otto von Habsburg, the last Hapsburg, is weighed down by 20 names, 15 of which are of saints, none of whom helped him to regain his throne.

Throughout history the church in Europe conferred and controlled the choice of names. That practice remains to this day in most European democracies, where pyramidal institutions control, monitor, allow or reject, enter and register the names of its tiny newborn citizens. England is an exception. There one can get away with a first name like Havana or Angola. Even in the erstwhile Soviet Russia one could have names like Stalen (Stalin + Lenin), Marlen (Marx + Lenin), and Elem (Engels + Lenin + Marx), the first name of the renowned film director Elem Klimov.

Southern Cyprus is predominantly Christian, although one does come across names like Aphrodite and Sophocles along with Georgios and Christina. However, the telephone directory has 16 pages (over 1,500 entries) of a very interesting surname: Haji (spelt 'Hadji'). A person who has been baptised in the Jordan River gets Haji attached to his or her surname, e.g. Maria Hadjisavvas and Christos Hadjiangou.

Not surprisingly, most Europeans are taken aback by names which have little to do with Christianity. George Mikes in his book *The Land of The Rising Yen* mentions that he carried visiting cards handed to him by Japanese acquaintances. The cards were Japanese on one side and English on the other.

'You point at a name and ask a Japanese friend what it is. He will say: Mountain Rice Paddy'.

'"Mountain Rice Paddy?" you ask slightly surprised. But it is Mr. Yamada's card'.

'Quite. But Yamada means Mountain Rice Paddy'.

One wonders what Mikes's reaction would have been to Indian names like Barkha or Megha (rain, cloud). But these are rather mild in comparison to some of the south Indian Shaivite surnames linked to the lingam, e.g. Shivalingam (Shiva's phallus) or Kamalalingaswami (the holy lotus phallus), Basavalingam (the bull's phallus) and Ramalingam. We have an infinite number of names, most still part of the active vocabulary, and new ones from all over the world being added daily. It would be an impossible task to compile them all into a single volume of 'acceptable national names', a requirement of numerous European authorities for permitting registration of a non-European name. Indians would take it amiss if their choices and decisions were curtailed and they were confined to a restricted list. Why can't there be a Dolly, Sanobar or Natasha Aggarwal, a Ram Rehman, Lenin Muralidharan or a Faqir Chand? And names, like plants, people and food, love to travel. Many Indian girls, born in the post-Second World War period, were named Zoya in memory of the brave anti-fascist Russian guerilla fighter. Che Guevara's girl friend's code name was Tanya, again inspired by Zoya's code name. In the 1950s, following Raj Kapoor's runaway hit *Awaara*, girls across the USSR were named Rita (Nargis's name in the movie). Incidentally, Uma Karuna Thurman, the famous American actress of Tarantino's *Kill Bill* film series, also has an Indian name.

A word of caution. Asian and African immigrants to European democracies, beware. Either rush back home for the baby's delivery or mentally adjust to your new homes where the state, in its wisdom, has a ready-made list of names for you to choose from.

22

The Tulips

◙

A profusion of red tulips dotted the velvet grass of the undulating Kazakh landscape, spilling over into the parks and avenues of Almaty. Wonderstruck, I asked a Kazakh lady about the whereabouts of a tulip nursery. She thought I was crazy — *'What Nursery! These grow wild'.*

I had never seen such an abundance of tulips and it took me a while to readjust my mind to the tulip's spatial and temporal associations. The arid regions of the Pamir, Altai and Hindukush mountains were the real home of tulips. The Emperor Jehangir, for instance, mentions that the residents of Kashmir grew them on their flat mud roofs and they looked spectacular. Tulips are indeed so elegant and beautiful that one can understand the Ottomans pining for their favourite flowers and dispatching messengers to the steppes of Turkestan to bring back bulbs for their newly-settled territories in present-day Turkey. Innumerable poems and songs have been dedicated to the tulip. It was believed happiness resided within the yellow tulip bud. Nobody could get it to open until one day a small child ran up to the flower laughing. It was the innocent laughter that made the tulip bud unfold its petals. Fizuli, the 16th century Azeri poet, in his famous poem, *Laila and Majnun*, describes the tulip's 'crimson cup' and 'ruby's glow' as the harbinger of spring. Majnun shares his secret with the tulips:

> Imploring all the tulips of the leas
> To tell his love in Leyla's pearly ear …
> He pressed the tulip's petals to his eyes
> And kissed its feet with lover's heavy sighs.

Once they had been brought from Central Asia to Turkey, tulip cultivation spread to all corners of the Ottoman Empire, to be grown by one and all, rich and poor. By 1726, the Ottomans had listed some 900 varieties of tulips and the Sultan's botanists had classified them with names such as *Ruby Drop*, *Matchless Pearl* and *Diamond Envy*. There was even a tulip growers' Handbook called *The Balance of Blossoms,* written by Sheikh Mehmet Lalezari, whose surname meant Golden Tulip. The image of this flower seemed to appear everywhere — in Ottoman miniature paintings, on royal robes, in carpet patterns, on tents and also on glazed ceramic tiles. There were even tulip-shaped fountains and vases. In the early 18th century the Sultan decreed a *Lale Devli* or the Tulip Period of festivity. It was a time for leisure, rejoicing and great creative activities throughout the Ottoman Empire. The Court Poet, Nedim wrote: 'Let us have fun, let us all dance and play, for it is tulip time!' Small wonder then that the tulip is Turkey's national flower. But then it also happens to be the national flower of Holland, the country synonymous with the tulip today.

The Europeans discovered the flower in the mid-16th century. In 1554, Ogier Ghislain de Busbecq landed in Istanbul as the Austrian Ambassador to the court of Süleyman the Magnificent. Busbecq wrote:

> We saw everywhere an abundance of flowers.... The Turks are so fond of flowers that even the marching troops have their orders not to trample on them.

But it was the tulip that really caught the fancy of the Austrian Ambassador. He returned to Vienna with some bulbs, which made their way first to Austria's Imperial Gardens. Some others he handed over to Carolus Clusius, a botanist. However, Busbecq got the name wrong. Instead of Lalé, he mistook it for the Turkish word for turban (tülbent). Thus the name — tulipano, tulipan and tulip! Now it so happened that in Holland some bulbs were stolen from Clusius's research garden, and overnight the tulip became a rage, but of a peculiar kind. Instead of poems dedicated to its elegance and beauty, people started betting on it, staking claims to it. The tulip was turned into a status symbol by the gentry and renamed the *Pot of Gold*. In 1634, Tulipmania or tulip madness broke out in Holland. D.G.Hessayon, a bulb expert, relates,

> Possessions of all sorts were sold to buy bulbs — a rare type could cost the price of a farm, house or coach and horses. Of course there were not enough bulbs to go round and so Tulipmania became a paper speculation.

Fortunes were made and lost till 1637 when the tulip bubble burst. Alexander Dumas's novel, *The Black Tulip*, is set in Holland at the time of the tulipmania where 100,000 guilders was the reward for cultivating the black tulip, 'a new flower, destined to bloom for one day, and to serve during that day to divert the ladies, the learned, and the curious.' The story of political intrigue and romance runs parallel with the author's critique of the tulip's commercialisation. Today Holland produces over nine billion tulip bulbs annually and a travel website invites tourists to enjoy the Dutch tulips in Kazakhstan.

✳

23

Chewing Rice for Others

▣

It might sound strange for us to be told by an Englishman, 'I'm afraid they are not available', or 'I'm afraid I cannot answer your question'. Would we then retort, 'What is there to be afraid of?'

Imagine the plight of translators who are involved in literary translations. There is a long list of imperatives for these poor souls. It goes without saying that it is imperative for the translator to excel in the two languages. I have read a translation in a publication: 'In her acorn fast moving eyes something always sparkled as if light was on'. Evidently the translator knew neither of the two languages.

The translator's knowledge of culture, history, economics, politics and social anthropology needs to be impeccable. Not only ought the translator be familiar with the specific work he or she is translating, he needs to be familiar with all the works of the writer and place the writing in the context of the literary movements of that period. In short, such a translator is no ordinary person but a genius. And if they were geniuses, why would they waste their time translating other peoples' works? All the more so if at the end of all the hard work they were to face some wise crack's retort that their translation resembles the underside of a carpet — the design is visible but the essence is lost. Even for the best translators it can be a frustrating effort to transcribe the subtle nuances of one culture into another. Take the case of Kumarajiva, a 4th or 5th century Indian Buddhist scholar who established a translation bureau in China to bring out 294 volumes in 11 years. Despite putting in this colossal work, Kumarajiva remained dissatisfied.

> The customs of Heavenly India lay great emphasis on literature. Her verses have developed a high quality of rhyming and rhythm, suitable for setting to music... When they are translated from Sanskrit into Chinese their elegance and beauty are gone. Although the sense has been conveyed the styles [of the original and translation] are extremely different. It is like to chew the rice in one's mouth and then feed it to others, not only the taste is totally lost, but it causes nausea.

Kumarajiva can be excused for his rather unpalatable comments, but they do convey the hardships that most translators encounter.

Let us turn to certain cultural traits of a given culture that have no parallels. One example is the description of an Indian beauty taken from ancient Indian literature.

'Lotus eyed, the colour of Champaka, and with the gait of an elephant'. In Sanskrit poetry a girl's eyes were beautiful if they reached her ears. As far as the elephant is concerned, the reaction of the Europeans at conferences has always been one of great amusement. In their perception, this enormous ungainly animal can hardly be considered graceful. My students' reactions too have been identical. In today's world this metaphor has lost its original meaning, and in this particular case the translator had to include a half-page commentary.

The same problem is inherent when we consider peculiarly Russian concepts, something that I am familiar with, like the image of the birch tree. This tree symbolises beauty, purity, grace and fragility. Russian poetry is replete with this metaphor, especially when describing a girl's beauty. Transposed into our context the birch tree does not evoke a similar emotional response. Should the translator opt for a coconut tree or a cypress? They might symbolise grace but not necessarily the other qualities. In any case, the cultural component is destroyed by this switchover.

I realise that most readers get confused with the multitude of Russian names in English translations. Take Tolstoy's *Resurrection* where the writer explicitly states that his heroine was, from birth, a victim of the whims and fancies of the two spinster sisters of the gentry who brought her up: 'She was called neither Katenka, nor Katka but Katyusha'. This one sentence explains volumes for the Russian reader for whom Katenka signifies affection, Katka is derogatory and Katyusha is neutral. The Hindi translation reads thus: 'Both the sisters called her Katyusha. This name was not so affectionate as Katenka, but, at the same time, not as derogatory as Katka.' With the insertion of this explanation, the translator has succeeded in conveying the subtleties of the name as well as the attitude.

But then, what about the Russian patronymics, which are appended to names to signify respect? Such appendages are absent in our cultures although the particle '*ji*' is attached to names as a sign of respect. Can the translator take the liberty of converting Alexander Nikolaevich to its Indian counterpart Sikander ji? Won't he fall into the trap of destroying the cultural image?

Fortunately, these unrecognised geniuses unobtrusively continue their work to spread understanding, love and appreciation of another culture through literature.

24

Repetersburg

⧈

This is about a city which has no night in summer and no daylight in winter, a city born of the whims of an individual, and built contrary to all commonsense, a city, like all cities, where governments are manipulative and ignore the sentiments of the inhabitants.

Peter the Great decided, one fine morning, that he wanted to be as far away from Moscow as possible. The reason was simple. The landed gentry and the clergy were not letting him have his way. So with a wave of his hand, he chose a spot for his new capital city on the shores of the Baltic Sea. But the site had bogs and marshes. Well, what are bogs for a Czar? Easily filled by colonised subjects and serfs who were in abundance. Italian architects were invited, and gradually the city of St Petersburg came up planned on a grid system. This was in 1703. For about 200 years it was to be Russia's capital. Each ruler added more grandeur to it. Palaces after palaces were commissioned. Italian architects Bartolomeo Rastrelli and Antonio Rinaldi brought in the Baroque style to the Winter Palace, now the Hermitage Museum.

Not surprisingly, the poet Pushkin commented that Peter had opened a window into Europe as the long Russian gowns were cut short to abide by French fashions, and beard tax was imposed on those who refused to part with their luxuriant facial growth. Miscellaneous German advisors were brought in and the Russian 'Pyotr' was substituted with the Germanic 'Peter' for the new city.

St Petersburg became an integral part of Europeanised Russia and an active participant in Russian fiction. 'I love you Peter's creation, I love your severe, graceful appearance'. This was Pushkin's city — of promenades and balls, of hope but also disenchantment, a city soon to be referred to as the Venice of the North. Nikolai Gogol's Petersburg emphasised the comic and the grotesque features, including a missing nose masquerading as a senior bureaucrat. In the latter half of the 19th century, St Petersburg became associated with Dostoevsky's city of the dispossessed, the insulted and the humiliated, a menacing, inhuman, artificial city with its dark alleys and coffin-like rooms. The First World War with Germany took the Czar by surprise. This was followed by rage. Nicholas II had to do something patriotic. He decided to change the name of his Capital. After all, 'burg' (in Petersburg) was derived from the German 'burgos' (town) as in Hamburg (incidentally, the Czar was part German by birth). Overnight Petersburg became Petrograd ('grad', 'gorod' the Russian equivalent for town), a name that lasted just ten years, up to 1924.

In 1917 the cruiser *Aurora* fired its historic salvo and Petrograd ushered in the age of Socialism. Three days after Lenin's death in 1924, the city was renamed Leningrad to honour the man who had led the Revolution. Nevertheless, there remained the stubborn ones and the dissidents who insisted on calling Leningrad 'Peter'.

'I was in Peter last month', or *'have you heard of the arrests in Peter'?*

Of course the dissidents were silenced while people continued to enjoy Leningrad's white nights. Then came the most tragic period in its history — the siege of Leningrad, which lasted 900 days from September 1941 till January 1944. The Germans surrounded the city with orders to destroy it and starve the inhabitants to death. When the siege began there was food and fuel rations sufficient for just a month or two. Leningrad was bombarded relentlessly for 900 days and turned into 'a dark city of weary survivors' who, against all odds, held out with extraordinary tenacity. During the siege, the Leningrad Radio Orchestra gave a live performance of Shostakovich's *Leningrad Symphony*, composed in 1941 and dedicated to the city and its inhabitants. It was performed by semi-starved musicians in coat sleeves, and was relayed through loudspeakers set up all over the city. In the same year, the Director of the Hermitage Museum, Orbeli, organised the 800th centenary celebrations of the great Persian poet Nizami. The message was clear — the human spirit cannot be destroyed. By 1944 almost a million civilians had perished.

Another 50 years went by and memories of Lenin were cast out. His enormous archive of classified documents tumbled out of the musty cellars to reveal more tales of horror. So the government decided, yet again, to reconstitute the city's identity by reverting back to Saint Petersburg. More chaos. Many inhabitants objected, protesting that it was Leningrad that they had defended against the Nazis, not Petersburg.

For now St Petersburg is the capital of the Leningrad Region, but if rumours are to be believed it could well be renamed Putinburg.

❋

25

Jokes Apart

The Cambodian driver of our hosts in Phnom Penh was laughing as he recounted how he had broken an enormous pedestal fan in the master bedroom. Two days later our host's car developed a snag on the deserted highway and had to be abandoned. The driver was telephoned and asked to do something: repair it, tow it back to town, or whatever. We squeezed into another car with friends and completed our sightseeing tour. Next morning the driver arrived.

'*Car broken*', he laughed, '*broken badly*', more laughter…

'Why have they employed this crazy fellow?' was my first thought.

'*Where is it now?*' the owner of the dead car asked.

'*In garage, for repair*'. More laughter.

Slowly the previous day's events were pieced together. Being a Sunday the driver was with some friends when he received the message about the car. He had no way of getting to the location, which was miles from anywhere. With great difficulty he managed to get to his brother in some village, where they borrowed a car and arrived at the site. It took them all evening and all night trying to resurrect the dead car. Finally they towed it back to Phnom Penh. He had just returned from the garage. All this was related, as you can guess, with peals of laughter. They had spent 14 hours with the car. Not one word of complaint. No sign of irritability. It was the narration of this story that finally unlocked the doors in my brain.

Year after year I had taught my students about different cultures and ways of approaching them. One of my favourite examples was about a Chinese gentleman who was late for an appointment with a foreigner — late by just ten minutes. With a big grin on his face he excused himself.

'I'm sorry I'm late. My mother just died'.

The foreigner was, naturally, horrified by the 'callousness' of the Chinese, just as I was when I listened to the Cambodian's tale of the broken pedestal fan. As outside observers we are baffled, mystified or simply misinterpret situations, far from comic, which provoke laughter in another culture. It is very easy to mistakenly conclude that both the Chinese man and the driver, who had broken the fan, were uncivilised and uncouth. Perceptions of etiquette vary from culture to culture. Laughter and smiles in countries of the Far East (China, Cambodia, Thailand, Tibet, Vietnam and others) do not signify only happiness or a response to something funny. Hiding grief or pain, embarrassment, loss of face or shame behind laughter is also an integral part of these cultures.

The man who lost his mother did not want to transfer his grief to another person. It was also a way of masking his sadness through a veil of smiles. The driver's laughter signified embarrassment and an apology for his clumsiness in breaking the fan. His laughter regarding the car ordeal was to make light of his work and not embarrass his employer.

Laughter as a display of affirmation and of life itself is, moreover, a prerequisite in most cultures across every continent. The earth, for instance is viewed as a female giving birth to produce. In many cultures, people, when sowing the seeds in spring, laugh and sing sexually explicit songs to encourage mother earth to be fertile and produce a good harvest.

I recall meeting a person in the Kullu district. He was explaining the local methods of preparing a home brew. The barley has to be spread out in a room and left to ferment. But before leaving the room one has to laugh heartily and loudly — a prerequisite for it to turn into good alcohol.

Laughter is magical. Flowers bloom with laughter. Amongst the Yakuts, laughter accompanies the birth of a child. Life and laughter are synonymous in the Togo myth of creation, for when god created a man and a woman the first thing they did was to laugh. Zoroaster is said to have laughed at birth. Similarly in the tale of Rustam and Zorab, the boy laughed the moment he was born. Koffi Kôkô, a well-known dancer from Benin in Western Africa, explains the connection between dance and laughter:

> Laughter is an exchange of energy. In these festivities, there is such an exchange of energy that people manage to forget themselves and to give the pure force they have within them. ... Laughter is vital for us. It preserves human nature. Laughing at ourselves, sometimes through others, is always positive.

26

Juvenile Delinquents

▣

The tiny village of Nako nestles at 12,500 feet in the folds of a gigantic mountaintop near the Indo–Tibetan border. Although life is not easy in this rugged terrain, the villagers always have a ready smile and tea for visitors. In recent years Nako has come into the tourist loop after the discovery of some exquisite wall paintings in its Buddhist monastery. One enterprising villager decided to build a seven-room hotel, the first in Nako. I accompanied a team of restorers who had booked some rooms in the hotel. On arrival we discovered that eight boisterous Israelis were, in fact, the new hotel's first occupants. The youngsters seemed very much at home. They spent their days lounging around in the dining hall, occupying all the chairs and tables, disregarding requests to make room for others. Their loud voices reverberated across the normally silent landscape. Then early one morning they vanished. They left Nako without paying some paltry sum for their seven-day stay. The owner, in a concerned voice, said, *'They must have had some problem. I'm sure they'll return and pay.'* They never did — not that year nor the following year. We know because we had to keep returning to Nako for the next two years.

Those Israelis were no exception. Today most shopkeepers, hoteliers, taxi or rickshaw drivers are reluctant to have any dealings with them. I gather India hosts thousands of Israelis annually. Ours is, by and large, a tolerant country, which even embraced the hippies of the 60s and the 70s. This is the first time that there is resentment towards one particular nationality. Nobody can say it is anti-Semitism because it is not. They are referred to as 'the Israelis'.

Not long ago a Jewish lady from England told me that Israelis are unwanted guests from Austria to the Philippines. There are even notices, she said, outside hotels in Vienna, with the words: 'No Israelis'. She explained away their aggressive behaviour with the argument that they were just out of the army and that they would mellow down once they joined the mainstream. It was a strange rationalisation. In my four-month stay in Palestine I have seen teenaged gun-toting Israelis dragging aged Palestinians out of buses because they were travelling without some imposed Israeli permit in their own land. Similar teenagers at Tel Aviv airport have abused me although all my papers were in order. How can such aggression, arrogance and, sorry to say, outright racism be suddenly transformed?

The English lady could not give me a satisfactory answer regarding Israeli school education. Why are they not taught about the lands that accepted them, lands where they did not face persecution? Aren't they taught that when the Jews were being persecuted in Europe and being burnt at the stake, it was Algeria, Morocco, Egypt, Iraq, Iran, India, the Arab world and Central Asia that had given them refuge? Where would they have been today without this support?

An Israeli designed an exhibition on Tibet in Dharamsala. It dealt with Chinese policies in the occupied areas, policies of dispossession, humiliation and torture, imprisonment and suffering. One had but to substitute the word 'Chinese' for 'Israeli' to grasp that the pattern was identical to the plight of the Palestinians. But that irony was lost on the designer who firmly upheld that Israeli occupation and aggression against people who have lived for centuries in Palestine is justified. Whenever I think of Israel I am reminded of Leo Tolstoy's prophetic words: 'We hate those whom we oppress more than those who oppressed us'.

There is also another side to it. These very youngsters throng to Buddhist meditation classes and Buddhist teachings in Dharamsala. A resident psychiatrist from Iceland in Dharamsala was relating her therapy sessions with a young traumatised Israeli who was suffering from an acute sense of guilt. He, as a commanding officer, it transpired, had stopped his subordinates from firing at unarmed Palestinian teenagers. No amount of counselling justifying his action as being correct could dispel his remorse for failing in his duty.

At home, we have a lethal memento from Israel. A marble-sized, so-called, rubber bullet. This 'rubber' bullet ricocheted off my husband's desk in Ramallah, where he had gone as a UN consultant on schools. It narrowly missed him. Had it hit him he would have been grievously injured. The 'rubber' bullet is part of the ongoing misleading Israeli propaganda because it is in fact made of solid steel. The Israelis have all along claimed that they use rubber bullets to fight the stone-throwing Palestinians. The rubber coating saves their conscience and supposedly justifies to the world the lethal assassinations that we read about daily in the newspapers.

The former Israeli Prime Minister Ehud Olmert's militaristic 'moment of truth' is offset by that of his daughter, Dana Olmert, of the Israeli pacifist movement that hopefully, one day, will become the voice of Israel's majority.

27

Earthquacks?

◙

Cats and dogs with tags around their necks that read 'I foretell the earthquake' were up for sale in an Armenian bazaar. The sales were brisk, but the timing was most inappropriate. This was 1998, and around 80,000 people had perished a few weeks earlier in one of Armenia's worst earthquakes. In its aftermath questions were raised, which were no different from the post-tsunami ones. Some contended that the early warning systems were inadequate; others felt that, but for the concrete jungles built in the 'seismic zone', the casualties would have been lower. The majority felt it was high time that people shed their apathy, turned to self-help rather than wait for governments and scientists to solve their problems. Many felt it was essential to rediscover the severed bonds with nature. And that is where the cats and dogs enter the picture.

One day before the earthquake a man in Armenia's Leninakan region noticed the unusual behaviour of his pet cat and dog. The next day, four hours before the earthquake, the cat sprang out of the building block and clambered up a tree, taking no notice of the mice below. The dog refused to re-enter the building, and instead, bit his master, who finally understood that something was amiss. He rang up the municipality, the police and the radio station, pleading with them to alert the population. His calls were met with scorn and ridicule. There were still two hours to go. Desperate, the man knocked on every door of his apartment building asking people to leave their homes. Four families complied. They were the sole survivors, who witnessed the collapse of their massive concrete housing complex which killed thousands. Their saviour had earlier lived for 20 years in the Kamchatka peninsula, a high seismic activity zone.

The 'miraculous escape' spurred a scientific research on the behavioural pattern of animals in the region prior to the earthquake. As was to be expected, all animals showed distinct behavioural changes, which ranged from restlessness to fear and panic as the time of the earthquake approached. Importantly, those in the epicentre region reacted as early as a month before the tragedy.

Science has established the close relationship between the earth and the moon's magnetic field, its links with live forms on earth. However, when it comes to the human beings' sensitivity and links to nature, these are shrugged off as superstition. One media channel welcomed the 2004 post-tsunami survival figures of some communities in the Andaman's but added, 'their death would have been a blow for anthropologists'. Four communities — the Shompen, Jarawa, Sentinelese and the Onge — survived by moving to high ground because they observed their traditional early warning systems, while others, like some Nicobarese who had become 'civilised', suffered enormous casualties. Similarly, the 80,500-strong Simeulues in Indonesia, despite being close to the tsunami epicentre, lost only seven people. Traditionally wise ways of seeing the movement of the ocean also helped Thailand's Moken or Sea Gypsies of the southern coast to survive. Communities across the globe which have been vulnerable to natural calamities have built up a vast body of wisdom to protect themselves.

Take Brazil's Amazon River, infamous for its recurring flash floods, and yet there are no human casualties. A researcher was astonished that communities living on its shores could, with uncanny accuracy, foretell the timing of the floods, and leave their homes well in advance. Finally, after 30 years of study, he stumbled onto the solution that could unravel the mystery. It was the ants. A week before the flood the ants would disperse in different directions. With great determination they would go about their 'data collection' and 'listen' to signals. After a day of such activity they had a 'round table conference of the 'meteorologists', followed by an exodus to higher ground. Did the locals follow the lead of the ants or were they independently sensitive to nature's early warning systems? A similar story comes from the shores of the Brahmaputra River whose annual flooding patterns are no less severe than those of the Amazon River. Before dams were built along this river, there were fewer casualties because the shore communities' understanding of nature had enabled them to find a balance between their life and that of the river. Their houses stood on stilts and withstood floods because traditional building techniques had been adapted to recurring natural calamities.

Likewise, ancient monuments and old houses, built with the time-tested wooden framework, survived the recent earthquake in Kashmir. Casualties were minimal amongst the Rawari community of Bhuj in the 2001 Gujarat earthquake. Their traditional houses protected them.

Happily, today there are people who are drawing on the experience of communities, generally ostracised by modern societies, but who have deep knowledge and wisdom about nature. One could recover traditional wisdom, learn from it and prepare oneself for calamities.

28

Crosswords

▣

Words fly with the winds. 'They slip away across the universe', transcending borders, bypassing visa and security officials, and sprouting, like seeds, wherever they find a fertile soil. They grow roots in a language long before dictionaries accord them an official status of recognition, or else seek to banish them.

Perhaps a hundred years from now, some linguist will come up with a 'theory' that American English is the mother of all languages by basing his assumptions on computer terminology which has reached every corner of the world. Hopefully by then people will not be as gullible as they were in the past and, while accepting the contributions, treat the 'findings' of the linguist as a humorous prank. The barrage of new computer terms is unprecedented: e-mail, floppy, mouse, spam, desktop, virus, hack, laptop, drag and drop, firewall — seemingly familiar terms with new meanings. And then there is SMS language. Every new technology comes with its peripherals — words.

Who can say that a particular language is pure with no foreign 'pollutants'? Throughout history, languages have been enriched by alien words through alien contacts. If the enrichment is transient, the adopted words soon fade into oblivion, but if crucial, they remain, come what may. They may even give way to new alternatives. Words like algebra, alcohol and elixir entered European languages a thousand years ago from Arabic and stayed on. Such words help us delve into a country's cultural history and pose uncomfortable questions to official histories.

The English ruled over us for just 200 years, yet observe the extensive spread of their language. Compare this to almost 800 years of Arab presence in Spain. It resulted in an even more significant influx of Arabic words in European languages, including in mathematics, science, astronomy and medicine.

As for the English language, by the 13th century it had adopted over 10,000 French words, 75 per cent of which continue to be used today. In 1066 the Norman king William the Conqueror invaded England and French became the official language of the English court, government and gentry. French terms relating to legislation, defense, fashion, food and much else wound their way into English and to this day English and French words coexist. There is 'freedom' but there is also 'liberty', 'wedding' and 'marriage'. 'Pig' is English, but its meat — pork — is French; 'cow' is English but 'beef' is French.

Governments, however, have unique ways of displaying their patriotism. The French Academy, originally set up in the 17th century by Cardinal Richelieu, has the responsibility to 'fulfill its traditional role of regulating language' by retaining the purity of French and expunging foreign words while inventing French equivalents. American English 'imports' are perceived as very dangerous viruses and they include the term 'e-mail'. To counter it the Academy has coined the term 'une letter electronique'. Perhaps the French government departments are perforce using this term, but ordinary people prefer 'e-mail'. France is not alone. I was informed by some German scholars that there is a German government handbook, a bible of sorts, with 'permitted' words. It is replenished every year. Despite language variations across Germany, the scholar/journalist has to limit his work to the permissible words through self-censorship, or else the editors and publishers will expunge them. India, Turkey and Pakistan did not want to lag behind Western democracies and they also made attempts to find equivalents for foreign terms. Occasionally foreign words and their government-sponsored equivalents coexist, but more often not, as in India. We have any number of irreverent rejoinders to our government's valiant endeavours to control language. People have offered their own substitutes for foreign 'pollutants' such as : *kanth langote* for 'necktie' — a literal, word-for-word translation — and *murg poonchhal sammelan* for 'a cocktail party'. The number of Sanskritised words incorporated into TV news assured the government channel of a dwindling viewership. Every time the news came on the air (in the days when there was only one channel) my uncle would declare, 'Now listen to Hindi in the News', *Ab aap samachar main Hindi suniye* (instead of '*Ab aap hindi main samachar suniye*'). A similar situation exists in Pakistan where I cannot follow the Urdu news on TV. There, the wise government has Persianised the language. Yet, chatting with friends on either side of the border poses no problems.

I personally prefer the freedom of multiple choices. If I want to express 'love', I want to be able to turn to *ishk, pyaar, prem*, love or *mohabbat*. Or do we need some erudite official to guide us in that as well? But there is always Bollywood to remind us what the winds have brought and seeded in our part of the world.

29

Food Traffic

回

I have received a *Pizza Hut* home delivery flyer listing the pizzas I can expect at my doorstep within half an hour. They include: *Veggie do Pyaaza, Paneer Pataka, Sabz Bahar, Killer Korma, Teekha Tikka and Chicken Toofani.* A detailed description of each pizza is included. *Teekha Tikka* is: 'succulent pieces of chicken *tikka* sit invitingly on a bed of onions and luscious mozzarella cheese', while Killer Korma is: 'a lethal combination of cheese, onions, green chilies and lamb korma'. Only one Italian ingredient finds a mention in the ingredients. To ensure sales, this food chain, which has 10,000 units in over 80 countries, has had to adapt its menus to suit our palate. Yet Italian pizzas were introduced some 30 years ago by our local food chain, Nirula's, and today the pizza base is available, like *naans,* off the counter in stores across Indian cities. Understandably, an Italian running an 'authentic' Italian restaurant in Goa was furious every time *Pizza Hut* was mentioned. '*How can people think that pizza comes from America?*' It was no use arguing with him that Italian migrants introduced this dish to America or that the term 'authentic pizza' could be a misnomer.

Not so long ago a newspaper reported that the fastest selling pizzas in the University area of Paris were those of an Indian roadside vendor who simply doled out *subzi* on to a *roti*. Closer to home, in Mayapur, the predominantly European adherents of the Hare Rama Hare Krishna sect run a vegetarian Pizzeria. Their religiosity extends to their pizzas, which are named after their central deity, Krishna: *Makkhan Chor, Hare Krishna* and *Gopala.* The person taking orders at the counter yells out to the cook, 'Two

Hare Krishna's with extra mozzarella, one *Makkhan Chor* with capsicum'. I wonder if their pizza range extends to the 108 names of Krishna?

Culinary authenticity is a myth. The staple diet of a region, which depends on its terrain and climate, coexists with food traffic and our taste buds keep adapting to new influxes. Alexander Dumas put it succinctly in his novel, *The Count of Monte Cristo*, a work that celebrates food traffic:

— *'Diable!'* he said, after having swallowed the divine preserve. *'I do not know if the result will be as agreeable as you describe, but the thing does not appear to me as palatable as you say.'*

— *'Because your palate has not yet been attuned to the sublimity of the substances it flavours. Tell me, the first time you tasted oysters, tea, porter, truffels, and sundry other dainties, which you now adore, did you like them? … Well, it is the same with hashish; only eat for a week and nothing in the world will seem to you to equal the delicacy of its flavour, which now appears to you flat and distasteful.'*

The fastest selling item in the UK, *chicken tikka masala*, is claimed as a British dish. London has over 8,000 Indian restaurants, apart from the hugely popular takeaways which outnumber the fish and chip joints. When an English tourist in India orders *chicken tikka masala* he is met with raised eyebrows: *'What do you want? Chicken tikka or chicken with masala?'* Another British creation is the much sought after mulligatawny soup, derived from the Tamil *'melagu'* (pepper) and *'tanni'* (water).

Then there is the American invention, American Chop Suey, a fried egg placed on top of noodles with ketchup. 'Chop Suey' is derived from the Cantonese *tsap sui* meaning 'odds and ends', and 'ketchup' originates from the Chinese Amoy language, *koechiap* or fish sauce. Culinary experts are also arguing over the origins of pizza. Some claim Etruscan or Greek origins, while others link it to the Middle Eastern *'pitta'* bread. But what about the pizza topping of tomato, or chillies, without which Asian food is inconceivable? Both come from South America.

In Japan I was asked to cook a meat curry, a hot favourite of my Japanese hosts. I prepared the best curry I was capable of, but it was disdainfully rejected by the gourmets, three Japanese kids. '*This is not Curry!*' They were indignant. The Japanese Indian meat curry is sweet. They add sugar to it to cater to the Japanese palate, which otherwise shuns sweet flavours.

Enmeshed in a web of cross-cultural fusion cuisine, people the world over continue to adapt, transform and re-create tantalising novelties to suit every palate. Today's world is one of spiralling food diversity and diversity of choices, and globalisation has only accelerated 'food travel'. The fast-food chains try in vain to standardise menus; in reality, one of McDonalds hottest selling items in India is *Aloo Tikki Burger*. While these global fast-food giants have been instrumental in the growth of indigenous food chains, they have also witnessed the assertion of local tastes.

30

Once Upon a Time

□

We were walking around parts of old Simla showing Giles, our English friend, the remnants of the Raj still visible as stray buildings along the Mall, a few ancient Deodars, odd cast-iron benches and the original Post Office. There was a time when no Indian, apart from the rickshaw puller, was allowed on this road. Winding our way back, we decided to stop at the Cecil Hotel, a massive concrete structure with marble and granite interiors, which had replaced the earlier stone-built Cecil. We agreed that all five-star hotels and airports look alike — faceless, synthetic and without history.

Still grumbling about the ugly changes, we headed for the bar tables at one end of the atrium. Before long a tall, corpulent elderly European made his way unsteadily to one of the tables using a walker. We had noticed him earlier in the lobby being helped out of a wheelchair. Now he was in the company of a young couple. Our grumbling gave way to concocting stories about strangers as we downed our refreshments.

'I bet he served in the British government and has returned with his grandchildren to relive his youth'.

The Englishman seemed quite at home, waving to someone while chatting and laughing with the hotel staff. Presently his companions got up to leave and the old man stood up on his wobbly legs and warmly shook hands with them.

'No, they aren't related. Chance acquaintances', we commented.

A smart young hostess came up to replenish our glasses. By now curiosity had got the better of me. *'Tell me, who is that old gentleman?'*

The girl looked back and smiled.

'He's English. He came in search of his house, Sherwood Cottage, where he lived between the ages of three and seven. He's 87 years old and has returned after 80 years. For ten days he searched everywhere. Yesterday he even went in his wheelchair all the way to Summer Hill but had returned so exhausted and dejected, that he was unable to eat anything.' Meanwhile, we were told, another search had also been conducted by the younger hotel personnel, all Simla residents, including the young hostess. Initially none of them had a clue where to start. The few remaining octogenarians gave them conflicting directions. Their last resort was the old Post Office. Its helpful staff dug out some moth-eaten registers, and finally, the morning of our visit, Sherwood Cottage was found. It was vacant and being painted for the next occupant. The hotel staff escorted the old man to his lost home, which he immediately recognised. His recall was astonishing. He remembered his room, the view from his window, his dreams, and the garden where he chased butterflies. He showed them the fireplace in the living room where he sat on his mother's lap while she read out bedtime stories to him.

His excitement had radiated and enveloped all the hotel employees who rejoiced at the successful denouement on the last day of his visit. What a tragic quest had he returned without tracing his home.

Our storyteller moved on. I sat in silence, speculating on his long and arduous journey alone in a wheelchair at the age of 87, on his precious memories that must have been so deep indeed as to pull him back to the Himalayas. Why is it that childhood memories often return to haunt us in old age?

Chuffed with ourselves that, apart from the detail concerning the 'grandchildren', we had not been too far off the mark, we paid our bill and left. A monkey, clasping her sleeping baby, was sitting on the ledge watching the passers-by. Our conjectures continued as we walked back to our hotel.

Giles said, *'I'm sure his family packed him off to a boarding school in England. He must have been miserable.'*

'You mean, his parents stayed back in Simla?'

'Yes, of course. Most families did that — sending their kids to good schools and good education back home. My wife's parents lived in Bombay and they put her on a boat when she was 7 years old. She was very unhappy in England and always held this grudge against them.'

We visualised the old man's childhood full of parental love and affection and how all this would have suddenly given way to terror as he was shipped off to a bleak existence in a strange country which was supposedly his own, but where he felt like a total stranger.

Add to it the English weather, which does not help either. Bleak, wet and cloudy days. The steel grey of the streets, the houses and the clothes…. and far, far away on the other side of the planet, him writing mandatory letters to an address where he had once chased butterflies in the sunshine.

❋

31

A *Tribute* ...

T he tram was moving at a leisurely pace along the main street. Presently an elderly man, sitting at the back, got up and headed for the front exit. As he slowly inched his way forward, one by one all the passengers stood up and bowed. That old man was Leo Tolstoy, a living legend and the voice of Russia's millions. He had become a crusader denouncing evil in all its manifestations — be it czarist autocracy or colonialism.

> I sit on a man's back, choking him, and making him carry me, and yet assure myself and others that I am very sorry for him and wish to ease his lot by any means possible, except getting off his back.

Most of his articles were banned for publication. Yet they were extensively copied, circulated clandestinely and printed abroad. People said Russia had two Czars — Nikolai II and Tolstoy.

> Who is more powerful of the two? Nikolai II is helpless against Tolstoy … whereas Tolstoy is forever shaking the throne of Nikolai and his dynasty. Let anyone lift a finger against Tolstoy and the whole world will be up in arms and our administration will turn tail and run.

Tolstoy's last novel, *Resurrection*, was a scathing attack of the government, the church and the judiciary. The authorities fought back and got the church to excommunicate him, hoping to ostracise and isolate him. The effect was just the opposite; spontaneous meetings and demonstrations of solidarity began. Tolstoy received thousands of telegrams of support. During the 1905 famine, Tolstoy set up relief kitchens in the affected areas while the Czar's government stood by in dumb silence. When the writer died in 1910, the demonstrators defied the government by taking up Tolstoy's slogan, 'Down with Capital Punishment'.

The belief in non-violence and love were the cornerstones in Tolstoy's later philosophy. Yet it was as a 19-year-old that Tolstoy had met a Buddhist monk who had revealed to him how non-violence was fundamental to every religion. Some believe that it was this meeting that spurred Tolstoy to join the Oriental Languages Department of the Kazan University. In later years he undertook a deep study of Buddhism, and then ventured into other Eastern philosophies, including the Vedas, the Indian Epics, the works of Vivekananda, Confucianism, Zoroastrianism and Islam. His readings convinced him of the truth revealed to him by the monk — that the essence of all religions, including Christianity, was that social change could only come from love and non-violence.

Just about this time in history, in 1893, a 24-year-old Indian arrived in South Africa only to be shocked by the rampant racism he encountered. A year later, he chanced upon some of Tolstoy's writings, but it was his most recent work, *The Kingdom of God is Within You* (1893), that overwhelmed him. '*It's reading cured me of my scepticism and made me a firm believer in ahimsa (non-violence)*'. Henceforth he regarded himself as a disciple of Tolstoy and named his commune 'Tolstoy Farm'. This young man was Mohandas Karamchand Gandhi. Gandhi's first letter to Tolstoy was in 1909. A brief correspondence followed. Tolstoy wrote to Gandhi how Christian nations had turned away from Christ's basic tenets:

> ... they deemed the use of force to be permissible, and based their lives on violence — so that the life of the Christian nations presents a greater contradiction between what they believe and the principle on which their lives are built: a contradiction between love ... and the employment of force, recognized under various forms — such as governments, courts of justice, and armies, which are accepted as necessary and esteemed.

Two months before his death, Tolstoy praised Gandhi's non-violent civil disobedience movement in Africa: 'Your activity is the most essential work, the most important of all the work now being done in the world.'

In 1915 Gandhi ji returned to lead India's independence movement by re-igniting its ancient principles of non-violence, which he had imbibed from his mentor Leo Tolstoy. Was it the completion of a circle or was it the birth of a simple idea that was to change the history of the subcontinent, South Africa and the USA? Gandhi ji's close associate, Khan Abdul Ghaffar Khan, or Frontier Gandhi, remained committed to his beliefs to the end. In 1955 this idea took root in America and Martin Luther King, popularly known as the American Gandhi, led 22 million American Blacks in a movement 'to end the long night of racial injustice'. Thirty-five years later a flame was re-ignited in South Africa when, after 27 years in prison, Nelson Mandela was released. His belief in non-violence had remained unshaken when he stressed, 'We must never lose sight of the fact that the Gandhian philosophy may be a key to human survival in the twenty-first century.'

The struggle to plant this simple yet profound idea, to ignite the small flame that feeds on the belief in renouncing force as a means of opposition, continues, be it Aung San Suu Kyi in Myanmar or Tibet's Dalai Lama. Indeed its relevance is anywhere where Imperial troops hold nations and communities to ransom because, as Gandhi ji said, 'Liberty and democracy become unholy when their hands are dyed red with innocent blood.'

32

Teri Mary Maa

◻

It took the Portuguese missionaries three long months of travel from Goa to arrive at Emperor Akbar's Court in Fatehpur Sikri. It took us less than three hours to fly from Delhi to Goa. Our drive from the airport was through lush greenery, the occasional dazzling white church or *girja* (our derivative from the Portuguese), and meandering rivers. The moment we crossed the bridge across the Mandovi River our taxi driver unbuckled his seat belt, removed the white shirt covering his bright orange t-shirt and announced with a grin, '*Traffic police left behind*!' He had had enough of Goan police regulations prescribing a seat belt and a white shirt.

Next morning we were reading the local newspapers in the German-run Lila Cafe recommended to us as the best place for breakfast in north Goa. The front-page headline read, 'Churchill Ridicules Faleiro's letter to Sonia'. Behind me I heard an Englishman exclaim, '*Imagine that! His first name is Churchill*!'

Churchill Alemao turned out to be the local Congress MP who was ridiculing Goan Education Minister Luizinho Faleiro's letter to the Congress President, Mrs Sonia Gandhi, concerning a new airport. Anything is possible in Goa. English surnames seem more attractive as first names, while Portuguese names jostle with a range of others.

To assume that Goan vitality was due exclusively to 450 years of Portuguese influence would only be partially true. One should not forget that Portugal was under Arab rule for 500 years. Consequently Goa received a heady mixture of Portuguese/Arab influences which, in turn merged with the rich amalgamation of local and foreign cultures already present in Goa from earlier times. Arab influences returning with the Portuguese included glazed tiles *azulejos* (from Arabic *al-zulayj*), *guitarra* or guitar and music, including *fado*. Catholicism arrived with the Inquisition.

An old friend, recently re-settled in Goa, dispelled some of our initial bewilderment. She is a Mangalorean Goan.

'The Mangalorean Goans are looked down upon by these fellows, who keep harping on about the good old days. Have you seen them in their black stockings in this heat? We call them PLOs...'

I thought of Yasser Arafat's Palestinian Liberation Movement.

'No, no, it has nothing to do with them. PLOs are Portuguese Left Overs'.

Many Goans, fearing confiscation of their property, converted to Christianity but continued with their earlier customs, dress and rituals. Relentless Portuguese persecution for their 'impure' practices finally forced them to flee to neighbouring Mangalore.

Seeing a large concrete cross, I asked my friend why there was a grave right outside her front entrance. But it was no grave. Like the sacred Basil or Tulsi plant found in brightly painted concrete containers outside Hindu homes, the converted Christians decided to place a cross for similar purposes. Most of these enormous crosses, scattered across Goa, are bedecked with garlands.

Next morning, we followed our friend's advice and looked up the matrimonial columns in the newspapers.

'GRCB Bachelor 27 yrs B.Com, 5'7 seeks alliance from GRCB Spinster, graduate, age 22/25 years fair, good family. Height 5'5'.

Why a 22-year-old girl had been referred to as a spinster was beyond me. Was it a Goan quirk? As for the acronyms, I might as well enlighten the readers: GRCB stands for Goan Roman Catholic Brahmin... but it could be GRCC as well with 'C' for *Chardo* or *Khatri*.

More letters can be added to these acronyms. There are Goan Saraswat Brahmin Roman Catholics (GSBRC), as well as Catholic Chitpavan Brahmins. Thus, depending on the situation, they can opt for a Goan identity at one moment, and at another a Christian or Brahmin one. They could also opt for all of them rolled into one, or something else altogether, for the dividing lines between these identities are so blurred.

As with all religions, in Goa too the earlier traditions and conventions got amalgamated into local innovations in the 'adopted' religion — like the crosses outside peoples' homes. One family, for instance, which looked after the local temple in a Goan village, continued to do so after being converted. This family was in charge of the church that had replaced the temple. In all likelihood they would have been the Brahmins.

Furthermore, the ancient (pre-Hindu) cult of the mother goddesses, the Saptamatrukas or the seven sisters, merged in time with the cult of Siva and Parvati, revered locally as Shanta Durga or Santeri, who later donned a Christian mantle as St Anne. The Cucumber Feast, for instance, is in honour of St Anne, the mother of the Virgin Mary venerated in Goa not only as St Anne, but also as the reincarnation of the mother goddess, Santeri. People of all faiths offer cucumbers to the goddess in order to be blessed with a child. Similarly, after Easter, all Goans celebrate the festival of Milagres Saibin — Mother of Miracles — in the Mapusa Church and both Christians and non-Christians offer oil and candles to the statue of Saibin, one of the seven mother goddess sisters. Such permutations are endless and preclude any attempt to box identities or cultures into pure hermetically sealed compartments.

✳

33

Size Matters

回

H ave you ever tried to turn the map of the world upside down? I have. It was an unnerving experience, which disoriented, confused and derailed my perceptions of reality. But soon confusion gave way to exhilaration at the prospect of being able to see the world in a totally new light. The Himalayas were now below me and Sri Lanka above.

This experience proved a simple point. Maps do condition the mind and shape our perceptions of the real world. A young Kashmiri boy who was asked about the size of England thought that it was larger than India. He was taken aback when he was told that England was just over half the size of his Kashmir, let alone India. However, going by the geography maps in school textbooks, his perceived reality was not too far off the mark.

Unfortunately school children all over the world have been taught with maps using Mercator's projection for generations. This map projection, developed in 1569 by Geradus Mercator, was meant for navigation across the seas. It seems, on the face of it, like an honest map that shows different continents, a map we take for granted and one commonly featured in most atlases and in flight magazines. Yet this map is misleading. Produced during a period of European expansionism, it understandably places Europe (Greenwich) at the centre of the earth. Earlier maps of the Chinese or the Arabs similarly projected their own regions at the centre of the earth. But there are other problems with the Mercator map.

Representing continents from the spherical surface of the globe on to a flat surface leads to distortion. It's a matter of choice which distortion is desirable. While Mercator's map shows the correct direction between two points on the globe, it enhances the shape and size of countries as you move away from the equator, especially Europe, which appears disproportionately larger than the equatorial regions. In Mercator's map, Greenland is bigger than Africa, which is in reality 14 times larger. Scandinavia is shown to be the same size as India although it is actually only one-third the size. The erstwhile USSR (22.4 million square km) seems bigger than Africa, which is 30 million square kilometres. Can we really blame the Kashmiri boy who gave an answer he had internalised from his school maps?

Realising the Eurocentric bias of Mercator's map, Arno Peter, the cartographer, made another one in 1974, which was 'fair to all countries'. His map is an 'equal area' projection as is Eckert's and Fuller's. In Peter's map, while the relative size of countries and continents is correct, there are distortions in the landforms [**Plate 11**]. Fuller's map shows the North Pole at its centre and locates all continents to the south.

Why is it then that we continue to fall into Mercator map traps? Is it just habit or inertia? Do these seemingly objective maps with an aura of scientific accuracy shape perceptions about ourselves? Does this perception of relative size influence others as well? Or are we overreacting?

Not long ago a young Brazilian I met in a London bookshop explained what he was doing in the UK.

'I used to study in the States but that place is so crazy that I decided to come here. Can you imagine, my teacher at college there asked me to describe life in Africa! I told her I was from Brazil. And she said, "Yes, I know, but how is it out there in Africa?" Unbelievable! My teacher — asking me about Africa! I decided to quit that country. Couldn't take it any longer. Now I'm studying at SOAS.'

For a long time America was comforted by two giant oceans that surrounded it on either side. But this tunnel vision has now exposed its vulnerability. In 1999 its President commented that Europe is a 'big country', and thought that Wales was in the USA. American children surveyed in 2006 by the *National Geographic* seemed not to lag too far behind their President. Six out of 10 did not know where Iraq, Afghanistan or Israel were located and almost half had no idea of the whereabouts of Mississippi State. Professor Alexander Murphy, former President of the Association of American Geographers, has in his recent article 'Awash in a Sea of Geographical Ignorance' commented that America is the only country where 'it is possible to go from kindergarten through university without a single basic course in geography. Some of our most prestigious universities do not even have geography departments.'

This isolation and deficiency of knowledge makes the ignorant population all the more gullible to government pronouncements. As far as we are concerned, perhaps the best way for us is to start afresh and refer to Peter's or Eckert's maps, turn them round and place the Indian subcontinent at the centre of the earth. Undoubtedly our self-confidence will soar to dizzy heights as we begin to regard Europeans as southern people. No longer will an island speck on the ocean, which once held us in captivity from above us for nearly 200 years, cow us down.

34

'Georgia on My Mind'

▣

Some countries attract one instantly. Georgia seduces you the moment you set foot on its soil: the snow-capped Caucasus mountains and the river torrents surging through its green valleys, the language which seems to echo the rivers with its multiple consonants that rain down on hapless tourists who struggle to pronounce the names of towns, rivers and people: Mtskheta, Mtkvari and Chkheidze... And then there are the Georgian people. In India a beautiful girl is often referred to as a Georgian fairy — *gurji pari*. And rightly so. This is a nation, famed for its handsome men and beautiful women, a nation that not so very long ago was in the forefront of artistic creativity. For me, however, it is the Georgian art of raising toasts that is unique. I have yet to come across any other place where a toast raised at a meal is sheer poetry. Inevitably it extends to psychology and the soaring heights of philosophy. This is a gift shared by one and all in this land of unlimited human love and generosity, a country of proud people, scintillating humour, delicious food, wine and *hamaams*. It is a country situated at the crossroads of cultures, a land whose shared histories and geographies embrace Persia, Byzantine, the Mongol Empire and the Arab Empire, and more recently, Russia. However, unlike many European countries, Christian Georgia had a long history of religious tolerance.

One name that turns up everywhere in Georgia's capital, Tbilisi, is Shota Rustaveli. Tbilisi's main street is named after Rustaveli, as is the National Drama Theatre, numerous parks, educational institutes, a metro station and even the highest government award in the arts. Shota Rustaveli was no politician. He was a writer who wrote Georgia's greatest classic, its most revered book — as important as the Bible. Till recently this classic was a mandatory gift for newlywed couples. Many Georgians knew its 1,600 quatrains by heart. *The Knight in Tiger's Skin* is an epic poem composed by Rustaveli in the 12th century, a hymn to love, friendship and the honour of commitment.

My curiosity got the better of me and I decided to read this poem, which the Georgians are so passionate about. Rustaveli dedicated the poem to the Georgian Queen Tamar. He writes: 'I have found this Persian tale, and have set it in Georgian verse'. Imagine my surprise when I discovered that one of the poem's principal heroes is an Arab. The poem opens with the Arab king, Rostevan, announcing his decision to abdicate his throne in favour of his only daughter Tinatin. There is much rejoicing. Later the king goes out hunting with his army chief, Avtandil. There in the distance he sees a handsome young stranger weeping who disappears when the king's men go to summon him. The king's happiness turns to sorrow at witnessing the suffering of another. Thereafter Tinatin asks her beloved, Avtandil, to find the mysterious stranger and promises to marry him on his return. Avtandil's long and arduous search finally leads him to the mysterious man, who is a knight dressed in a tiger skin. I was in for yet another surprise. This mysterious stranger, this elusive knight turned out to be an Indian prince by the name of Tariel. His tragic tale is recounted. We learn that his father gave Tariel up for adoption to a neighbouring Indian king who was childless. Later this king had a daughter. Tariel and his adopted sister, Nestan-Darejan fall in love.

But there are calamities and she disappears, leaving him inconsolable at her loss. Avtandil swears his friendship to the Indian prince and vows to find Tariel's beloved even if it means sacrificing his life. The narrative goes on to describe Avtandil's search and encounters, the help he receives from people of different nationalities, and the happy denouement. Tariel is reunited with Nestan and they return to rule India. Avtandil, having successfully completed his mission, marries Queen Tinatin. Two mighty heroes — one Arab, another an Indian. The story unfolds in the vast landscape of Arabia, India, Khorezm and numerous imaginary lands. There are references to Persia, China, Egypt, but not a word about Georgia. Rustaveli refers to the Koran, Mecca, Easter and Navroz; alludes to Rustam of Firdausi's *Shahname* and to Nizami's *Laila-o-Majnun*.

Not only is the tale a fusion of cultures, but even the poetic genre chosen by the author is eclectic. Persian and Arabic imagery abound in the poem, such as the rose as a metaphor of beauty, love and purity. There are numerous Sufi concepts and imagery such as *khanaqa, ashiq, majnoon*. The poem's verse form — known in Georgian as *shairi* (derived from the Arabic) — consists of 16 syllabic quatrains, each with a single rhyme. Popularised by Rustaveli, it remained the basic metre of Georgian poetry till the 18th century.

Rustaveli celebrates life in all its beautiful aspects. His celebration goes beyond borders for it searches out riches no matter where they are located, and from these diverse cultures he gifts to Georgia its unique epic.

✳

35

The 'Civil' Servant

◳

A young ambitious bureaucrat wakes up one morning and reaches for a mirror to check the pimple on his nose. Much to his horror he discovers that his nose is missing! Instead of a nose there is a smooth patch between his cheeks. What is he to do? *Uski to naak kat gayi.* How untimely for his career and marriage prospects to a girl from a wealthy family! With a handkerchief covering the vacant spot, the bureaucrat rushes out of his flat, and suddenly he sees his nose alighting from a grand carriage. It is wearing the uniform of a very senior bureaucrat. Our hero is at a loss as to how to approach his senior. Finally, summoning up enough courage, he goes up to the Nose and timidly mutters, 'Good Sir, you ought to know your place'. The Nose contemptuously examines this low-ranking bureaucrat who insists on accosting him, turns away in disdain, and departs in his carriage. Our hero then tries unsuccessfully to place an advertisement in the newspaper about his missing nose that is masquerading as a high official. He rushes to the police to lodge a complaint, but the guardians of law, as is to be expected, refuse to write down the complaint Our young bureaucrat is up against a heartless state machinery.

So the story continues, with many bizarre twists and turns as its author, the 19th century Russian writer Nikolai Gogol, revels in unmasking the bureaucracy. How wonderful it is to be able to laugh at this universal species. Most of the time we tear our hair out in frustration, and run around in circles, unable to find a way of getting around these 'servants of the people'. Rather, we are made to feel guilty for disturbing the seemingly overworked armies of bureaucrats. Even when we go into a bank where our life's savings are kept for safe keeping we are regarded as potential criminals who are being granted favours for daring to approach and claim some form or draw our own money. Bureaucrats are the same everywhere, whether they be diplomats of foreign missions or immigration officials at airports. They peep out of every crack in the edifices they inhabit. No wonder the term 'bureaucrat' has acquired a negative connotation.

Is there a way out? My thoughts turn to another era in another country where I imagine this idyllic utopia of gentle, thoughtful souls who go out of their way to serve society. China was once such a place, famous from ancient times as a nation of poets. 'What has poetry to do with bureaucracy?' you might ask. Let me explain.

During the golden age of the Tang dynasty (AD 618–907), civil service examinations were held to select future administrators. Indeed, it was China that first introduced the civil service exams we know so well now. One of the major components of the exam syllabi was poetry composition. It was the emperor who selected the best candidates. Thus it came about that many renowned Chinese poets were also high-ranking government officials. Poetry was so important that as far back as 3,000 years ago, the Chinese government appointed officers from amongst 'men above sixty and women above fifty who were without children', to collect poems from the population at large in order to get a feedback on the government's functioning. These officers were known as *shiguans* (poetry officers).

> The ruler patronizes poetry and poetry criticizes his mistakes. Those who criticize are not guilty. The one who is criticized should take lesson from it.

We desperately need poets as bureaucrats. Imagine if we had such civil service exams and every third bureaucrat was a modern day Ghalib or Amir Khusrau, a Rabindranath Tagore. Imagine if our officials were enlightened and sensitive souls. What courtesy and politeness they would show us and what care they would take to solve our problems. Our trips to their offices would turn celebratory.

But let us not despair. At least we now have the RTI or the Right to Information Act which is about public accountability with every citizen having the right to inspect government files on any matter that concerns the public. (If the file is not made available to the citizen, the official faces punishment.) This isn't necessarily going to make poets of officials, but the first step has been taken.

36

Devotion

□

It took a lot of persuasion from me to get her to return to the site, but finally Bayan relented. She hadn't visited Yasawi's mausoleum for five years, not since she had quit her job there. But so intense was her attachment to the monument that immediately on our arrival there she was excitedly explaining its history and the fate of those who undertook to restore the enormous 14th century Timurid monument. Built over the great Sufi Saint's grave, she recounted its bombardment by the Czarist colonial army in 1864; the beginning of the restoration work in 1951; and the role played by four women conservationists to recover this ruin [**Plate 12**].

The story of its restoration began in 1951. That year, a Georgian deportee, Tina Karumidze, was brought to the site by the Kazakh authorities. They had discovered from her documents that she was an architectural restorer. So they got permission from the KGB to let her work on Yasawi's bombarded tomb. One may well ask what the KGB has to do with restoration and that too in Kazakhstan. Tina Karumidze was one of many deportees at the time who were flung across Soviet territories. Her guilt was that she was the 'wife of the enemy'. Her husband, an important Communist Party functionary of Georgia, was shot dead during the Stalinist purges. Their children were packed off to an orphanage.

Despite her enormous personal tragedy, or maybe because of it, Tina Karumidze immersed herself in the restoration work. With almost superhuman energy she analysed and meticulously documented the construction details of the entire Yasawi structure. Finally, having understood the monument, she began to restore the main facade that had been badly damaged by the Czarist canons. Although she only worked on the site for four years, she left behind a wealth of documented material, notes and guidelines in her diaries. These diaries that she filled meticulously over innumerable hours formed the basis for all the subsequent restoration work that was carried out in the next four decades. Her sudden departure for Georgia in 1954 was prompted by the death of Stalin and her release. She hurried back to search for her children.

Lyudmila Mankovskaya, who continued the work of restoration with equal passion, succeeded Tina Karumidze. She further unravelled the keys to understanding Timurid architecture. Using the original 1397 text of the *Zafar Nameh*, which recorded Timurlane's visit to the site, she unearthed the proportional system that Timur's builders used to define the geometry of the monument, illustrating how the mausoleum was a virtual catalogue of Timurid construction practices. She was succeeded by Sofia Tukebaeva who focused her research on Timurid ceramic glazes. Much of her work was undertaken at the kilns where she often spent over 30 hours at a stretch. These long hours near the furnaces led to her untimely death in1992. Bayan Tuyakbaeva and her husband, Alexei Proskurin, had joined the project in 1968. They spent the next 30 years of their lives committed to its conservation. Bayan researched the epigraphy and decoded the carpet-like geometric patterns on the façade as a form of Kufic calligraphy. Thus, missing and damaged words were restored. Work slowed down in the 1980s due to lack of funds. But not for long.

The age of devoted restorers gave way to corporate contractors when in 1991 the Turkish government offered the newly established state of Kazakhstan 17 million dollars for Yasawi's restoration. A Turkish construction company moved in to ostensibly work in tandem with Tuyakbaeva and Proskurin. But there were frequent changes in the Turkish team and a lack of sensitivity to the peculiarities of Yasawi. This led to tensions between the Turks and the Kazakhs. The enormous budget for the project and the money being spent on it attracted sharks. Many people suddenly became interested in the restoration project, including the local mafia. Tuyakbaeva realised that the funds meant for restoration were being misused, and saw 40 years of restoration work trashed as modern factory tiles began to cover the dome and new materials being introduced to speed up the process. When she could bear it no more, she sent off letters of protest to the President and to Parliament. An inquiry commission was set up. But she had become dispensable and faced reprisals from the protected mafia. One day her briefcase full of precious documents was stolen, and then an attempt was made to set her home on fire. Undeterred, Bayan Tuyakbaeva continued with her own work on Yasawi. But when her 17-year-old daughter was kidnapped she finally gave up, quit work, recovered her daughter and sent her out of the country. Proskurin continued to work with the Turkish team, though with growing sadness, for another two years but a heart attack put an end to his engagement with the project. Today Yasawi's mausoleum with its shining tile dome appears on every Kazakh bank note as the most important symbol of Kazakhstan's heritage.

✳

37

Authentiques

◙

Our neighbours on Koh Samui Island were a French couple. The wife, with her Cleopatra hairstyle, was a professor and her husband a painter. They adored India, having visited it over 20 times. Both lamented the theft of ancient Asian art treasures that were ending up in foreign antique markets. We also agreed and deplored the recent thefts from the Kabul and Baghdad museums.

'*Fortunately*', I added, '*this region, including India, has retained an unbroken tradition of image making that is still alive and kicking.*'

'*Every period has its own energy*', the painter responded, '*but today's sculpted Ganesha lacks the energy of earlier times.*'

I smiled. '*Swamimalai in Thanjavur has continued with its ancient tradition of metal casting where great sculptures are still made. For them the act of creation remains devotional. As for energy* I continued, *every age has masters and mediocrities. Just because it is beautiful doesn't necessarily mean that it is ancient.*'

The painter's wife joined in: '*What wonderful Natarajas there are in the Madras Museum. Incredible! But the Museum! Its is in an awful state — unkempt and empty.*'

We were getting into dangerous waters but I persevered and told them that 'the museum' was a European invention and that often non-Europeans are unaccustomed to seeing fragments of their cultural artefacts displayed in glass cases. After all, museums were created as sanctuaries for the looted treasures of colonial plunders. The Europeans of course believe that they saved these treasures from destruction and kept them safely in their museums for posterity. However, what they created was a market for collectors, which is being fed by rampant thefts of antiquities by our own citizens to feed the antique markets of the West. It is a vicious circle of collectors' greed and the thefts needed to feed it, leading to more greed and more thefts.

My impassioned explanations seemed to have fallen on deaf ears, for a little later, the French artist brought a collection of photographs of Buddhist statues. He sought our help in deciding which ones to buy from the Bangkok dealer on his return journey home. There were some exquisite pieces from Cambodia, Thailand and Burma. We pointed out our favourites, but warned him that preferences are always very personal. We had no idea of their antiquity. His professorial wife suddenly intervened, '*I tell him we need a new car, but he prefers to spend the money on a Buddha. He has so many of them at home.*' Later we berated ourselves for helping them smuggle out antiques since the dealer had assured the painter that some of the images were very old.

On the day of our departure, the French couple told us about their chance meeting with a Chinese gentleman who ran a restaurant and how, before he had ventured into the restaurant business, he had run a lucrative sculpture and wood carving workshop in Bangkok specialising in 'making antiques'. But he had left that business because his conscience would not allow him to turn faith into profit. According to him, all the 'antiques' being sold in Thailand were new. Each one of them! Our friends seemed dejected but cheered up a little when their new acquaintance promised to examine their photographs the following day.

This incident reminded me of our visit some years before to the famed Kishangarh miniature painting workshops of Rajasthan. Many artists were at work and we were shown the various stages of preparing the paintings, which was primarily a collective endeavour. At the end of our tour we were taken to a small room where our painter guide pointed to the floor and said, '*This is where we antique them*'. Seeing our questioning looks he threw a recently completed painting on the mud floor, placed his foot over it and violently scraped it into the mud.

'*How can you do this?*'

'*Ji, that is what the foreign tourist wants. Antique. So we give them the antique*'.

Two days after leaving Koh Samui we were doing the rounds of the Angkor Wat temples with their missing and headless statues. The explanation was provided in a constantly replaying video in the hotel lobby showing photographs of the young Andre Malraux (later to become the French Minister of Culture), caught stealing enormous carved columns from the Angkor temples and transferring them to a huge river barge.

I worried about how many of those stolen treasures were now in museums and private collections in France or other parts of Europe. But then one wonders too about how many tourists have been outwitted by today's geniuses who continue the ancient carving traditions in India, Burma, Thailand and beyond? Who will have the last laugh? Are today's works of sculpture less authentic than the 2000-year-old ones? One European restorer claimed to me, while looking at a Buddhist mural, that she wanted to scrape the 800-year-old paintings to get to the 'authentic' 1000-year layer underneath.

Questions about authenticity in art will stay with us for a long time with little hope of resolution.

38

To The Holy Pope

▣

Dear Papa ji

I greet you as a learned Pope, a veritable encyclopaedia on ecclesiastical matters, blessed with a sharp memory which you have demonstrated recently by quoting a 14th century text from the millions of books and manuscripts in your Vatican Library. I am not writing to remind you about the roasting of non-Christian souls during the days of the Holy Roman Empire, or the enthusiastic work of your Jesuits in pursuing something you call the Inquisition. I also promise not to embarrass you too much by reminding you, dear Papa ji, about the sacking of Byzantine's Sancta Sophia by French Crusaders in AD 1204.

I must confess that when you made your remarks quoting a Byzantine Emperor of the 14th century, I rushed to my tiny shelf of books to learn more about your disquietude. I tried to understand the reasons why your wise predecessors in the Middle Ages chose to make a beeline for Spain, the hub of 'infidel' Islamic territories, to study with the infidels, to learn the Arabic language, to translate works from the Arabic, and to even set up institutions on the lines of Arabic ones. Do allow me to tell you about two instances.

At a time when medieval Europe was steeped in illiteracy, a French ecclesiastic named Gerbert d'Aurillac (945–1003) headed for Moorish Spain. You would agree, Papa ji, that this should have been the last place a cleric should go and become a victim of temptation, considering the warnings of the 9th century Spanish writer, Alvaro de Córdoba, who had written:

My fellow-Christians delight in the poems and romances of the Arabs; they study the works of Mohammedan theologians and philosophers, not in order to refute them, but to acquire a correct and elegant Arabic style. Where today can a layman be found who reads the Latin Commentaries on Holy Scriptures? Who is there that studies the Gospels, the Prophets, the Apostles? Alas! The young Christians… have no knowledge of any literature or language save the Arabic; they read and study with avidity Arabian books; they amass whole libraries of them at a vast cost, and they everywhere sing the praises of Arabian lore. … at the mention of Christian books they disdainfully protest that such works are unworthy of their notice. The pity of it! Christians have forgotten their own tongue, and scarce one in a thousand can be found able to compose in fair Latin a letter to a friend! But when it comes to writing Arabic, how many there are who can express themselves in that language with the greatest elegance, and even compose verses which surpass in formal correctness those of the Arabs themselves!

Now this Frenchman, Gerbert, chose to study mathematics, astronomy, physics, music and of course Arabic. On his return he introduced these new subjects in the cathedral school in Rheims. Gerbert's acquired Moorish knowledge was so impressive that he became the tutor to the Roman Emperor Otto III and Pope Gregory V. This scholar, who had obtained his learning from infidels, eventually became Pope Sylvester II (999–1003). But such erudite people were too far ahead of their times for after his death, rumours spread that he had sold his soul to the Devil and practiced sorcery. Gerbert's attempts at introducing Indian numerals and astronomy were similarly swept under the Vatican carpets for a few more centuries.

You must be aware, Papa ji, that Pope Sylvester was not an aberration. In the 10th century, when the church was setting up schools, your clergy was encouraged to go and study and translate at the Moorish centres of learning. By the 12th century there were hundreds of Christian clerics flocking to Toledo for studies. No doubt you know about Adelard of Bath, Gerard of Cremona and so many others.

Another of your illustrious predecessors in the 16th century was Papa Leone X, who ostensibly arranged a kidnapping in 1518.

Famous in your history as a patron of art and artists, including Raphael, it was Leone who enlarged the Vatican Library. The kidnapped victim was brought to Pope Leone who baptized him, christened him with his own name, made him teach Arabic to the Vatican priests, and asked him to write a geography of Africa — for centuries the only sourcebook on Africa for the Europeans. The book's author was al-Hasan al-Wazzan or Leo Africanus. After the death of his papal patron, Leo Africanus escaped from Italy and returned to North Africa, once again a Muslim. Do please read his story written by Amin Malouf, a Lebanese Christian writer of our times, who celebrates the wonders of diversity and emphasises inclusiveness and tolerance.

One last thing, Papa ji: your remarks confuse me because I don't see what religion has to do with anything you said. For centuries a Palestinian Muslim family has had custody of the key of Christianity's most revered shrine, the Church of the Holy Sepulchre, the site of Christ's Crucifixion and Resurrection. Every morning the head of this Muslim family unlocks the door and every evening locks it — a ritual intended to maintain peace amongst the various Christian sects.

✳

Linguistic Creativity

◉

With the hoardings overpowering the streetscape announcing in Roman script '*HIT HAI*', it did not take long for our purists to bemoan '*Hai, Hai*' about the use of Hinglish (Anglo-Hindi) and a foreign script.

It is difficult to understand why people get so agitated about new ways of conveying ideas, especially since scripts, like languages, are in a constant state of flux and throw up so many choices. My grandfather's generation, for instance, studied Urdu and Persian and wrote Punjabi in the Urdu–Arabic script. Prem Chand, the father of contemporary Hindi literature, wrote his first works in the Urdu script and subsequently turned to Devanagiri. My father's generation was proficient in both Urdu and Devanagiri scripts. As a writer, my father wrote in Hindi, Urdu and English, and wrote Punjabi in the Devanagiri script, as did his actor-brother who, in his later years, learnt the Gurmukhi script.

Problems arise only when governments and fundamentalist groups jump into the fray and unfortunately start equating scripts with a religion or with human progress, and follow it up with the imposition of a particular script as in the case of Turkey and the former Soviet State.

Left to ourselves and in the absence of government directives, we are indeed happy to embrace scripts and languages freely, adapting them to suit our needs.

Linguistic creativity is at its best in the advertising slogans for the English-speaking middle class. For instance, Dabur sells 'Lal Tail' (Red Oil), a road sign invites you to have 'Child Bear' (chilled beer) and 'Aloo Chat' (chaat), and one brand of *haazma* pills is called 'Gas Go'. Another common one is seen on trucks where 'Liver Box' announces the location of the Lever Jack.

When we transfer our languages into Latin script, both sounds and meanings can change. Occasionally even people's reputations are endangered. The painter Chain Prakash should have stuck to the Devanagari script because his name inadvertently metamorphosed from 'patience' to 'chain' in invitation cards. Script crossover has its own amusements. The English alphabet simply does not offer the range of sounds of the language it is transcribing. When we write 'yoga' instead of 'yog', or karma instead of 'karm' in English, we end up pronouncing these words as yogaa and karmaa, instead of the Sanskrit pronunciation of the short 'u' sound ending as in 'but'. I have heard diplomats complaining about their embassies being located on a rather disagreeable sounding road in Delhi and they wonder whether the Indian government is enjoying a private joke at their expense. 'Shanti Path', or 'Peace Avenue' when pronounced with an American accent reads as 'Shanty Path'. Bilingual interfaces can also lead to hilarious mix-ups. Now 'Deep' is a popular name in the Punjab and means light as in *diya* and Deepawali, the festival of lights. Hardeep and Gurdeep are common Punjabi names. When pronounced, the 'd' is a soft sound, closest to the English 'th' as in 'the'. But such subtleties have never deterred the full-on Punjabi. Boards along the Chandigarh Kalka highway announce locations for 'Deep Abortion Clinic', 'Deep Dentist', and 'Deep Piles Clinic'.

Then there is the case of Dera Bussi, a small town in the Punjab where the signboard in English changes Bussi to Bassi. The mandatory liquor shop on the highway is called 'Bassi Beer' (stale beer) and Bassi Gas is where the gas cylinders are available. In all these instances our scripts are also present to guide us back to the fold of *'desi'* pronunciation. Moreover, being multilingual, people of this subcontinent are in perpetual translation mode and can enjoy these linguistic shifts and puns.

The voluminous thousand-odd-page Hobson-Jobson dictionary of 1886 illustrates the phonetic transformations that occurred with words the British adopted from our regions: *'bangla'* becoming bungalow and Kashmeer becoming Cashmear. Both grammatical borrowings and sound transformations can occur in the recipient language. I came across a pub in Moscow called Monksy i Naansy. It took me a few moments to realize that it stood for 'Monks and Nuns'. The words had double plural endings, both English and Russian.

It is not rare for users of a foreign language to resort to features of their own language while speaking or writing. There can be entire sentences where the grammatical structure or the order of words of the native language exerts its rights in translation, for example, a notice outside a temple in Bangkok states: 'It is forbidden to enter a woman even a foreigner if dressed as a man'. Outside a cemetery in Moscow, a notice reads: 'You are welcome to visit the cemetery where famous Russian composers, artists, and writers are buried daily except Thursday' [**Plate 13**].

All said and done, it is so good to laugh and appreciate the attempts made by peoples to reach out to each other. And now, outsourcing to Indian call centres, has produced a new breed of typists who save European money and time by processing information in India. I leave you with a medical example of 'Eustachian tube (in the ear) malfunction' which was transcribed as 'Euston station tube malfunction'.

�֎

40

Paper Trails

The Chinese traveller Chou Ta-Kuan was horrified by some Cambodian customs:

> After visiting the privy they always wash themselves, using only the left hand: the right hand is kept for use at meals. When they see a Chinese cleaning himself with paper at the privy, they jeer at him and indicate their unwillingness to have him enter their homes.

Only a Chinese could express surprise at somebody not using toilet paper as late as 1296 because they had invented paper in the 2nd century BC. Mr. Chou Ta-Kuan's baggage, no doubt, included other Chinese inventions already in wide circulation like multicoloured printed paper currency, printed books, newspapers and even playing cards for recreation.

Today, the multiple uses of paper are taken for granted, while science keeps predicting that computers and the Internet will make paper redundant. Nothing could be further from the truth. More paper is wasted today than ever before. Yet undoubtedly this Chinese invention of turning the pulp made from mulberry tree bark and hemp rags into paper was equivalent at that time to the Internet revolution of today. Like the World Wide Web, paper too caused a similar explosion that scattered knowledge across the globe, and continues to do so 2,000 years after its invention.

The best thing about paper is that it can be preserved. In the early 20th century, over 30,000 ancient paper scrolls were discovered in Dunhuang (China) and Penjikent (Tajikistan) that dated back to the 4th to 10th centuries. These scrolls were scripted in

Uighur, Chinese, Sanskrit, Persian, Tibetan, Arabic and Soghdian, indicating the widespread use of paper in Asia along the Silk Trade Route. When paper-making spread to Korea and then to Japan, they refined it to a fine art as they do to all things. They produced paper clothes, parasols and even wall partitions to counter earthquakes in Japan.

Paper's journey to the West was rather slow. The Europeans followed 1,400 years after the Chinese started making it. But the journey itself was eventful. In AD 751 a group of Chinese paper-makers were kidnapped and taken to Samarkand, where a paper-making unit was set up. Soon Samarkand paper, made in six different varieties, was unrivalled for its quality. Al-Khorezmi jokingly complained that his friend did not write to him because he lived too far from Samarkand and must have found paper very expensive.

After Samarkand it was the turn of the Arab Empire to establish a paper mill in 794 in Baghdad, followed by one in Syria and a century later in Egypt. An 11th century Persian traveller to Cairo was taken aback at the sight of vendors freely using paper to wrap vegetables. By the end of the 12th century, Morocco had over 400 paper mills. In Fez, it is said, there was a mosque with beautiful gold ornamentation. Fearing it would be destroyed by the strict orthodox conqueror, Abd al Mumin of the Almovads, the residents of Fez covered the ornamentation over with white sheets of paper. The ploy worked.

Paper was indispensable for the great centres of learning in the Arab Empire. Works were being written on a variety of subjects from cookery to botany, history, fiction, astronomy and optics, and placed in the great libraries of the Arabs. By the 9th century, it is said,

> While paper was still an unknown commodity in the West, the Great Library in Cordova had about six hundred thousand manuscripts. There were also bookshops and more than seventy other libraries.

Finally, in the 12th century, paper-making reached southern Europe. The first paper mills were set up by the Arabs in their

Spanish and Italian domains. As paper travelled westward, so did its names and terms. Early Arabic and Turkic words for paper — *kaghad* and *kaoit* — are derived from Uighur and Soghdian words which in turn are from the Chinese term *gu-zhi* (mulberry bark paper); and that is the source of the word *kaghaz*. From the Arabs we also got their most common term for paper, *waraq*, which today is associated with the thin coating of silver leaf on *paan* and sweets. The term 'ream', the equivalent of 500 sheets of paper, taken from the French *rayme*, which is from the Spanish *resma*, is in turn a derivative of the Arabic *rizmah* (bale or bundle).

Printing on paper is another story. It takes us from the oldest surviving printed book — *The Diamond Sutra*, a Chinese Buddhist text of AD 868 — on to the mid-15th century when the first European (Gutenberg) press adopted the Chinese and Korean moveable-type block printing technique. Amongst the earlier printed books in Europe were those by non-European scientists. Between 1500 and 1550, for instance, the Latin translation of Ibn Sina's or Avicenna's *Canon of Medicine* underwent 30 editions. It was a mandatory textbook in Europe's medical colleges till the 17th century. The first Arabic edition of the *Canon* was printed at the Medici Press in Rome in 1593.

✳

41

You're in Safe Hands

◉

S he gently took my left hand and placed her fingers on my wrist. A few moments later she repeated the gesture with my other wrist.

'*Oh dear, she can't find my pulse*', I thought.

I was watching her. Her eyes were shut, her head inclined to one side. She was in another realm. Finally she looked up and said, '*You got up too soon after a Caesarean operation and are going to suffer back problems.*'

Well folks, I did indeed have a Caesarean and I had got up too soon. But the fact of the matter was that there I was wearing a thick sweater, my son was already four years old and importantly, till that moment I had not uttered a word.

'*Right now I do not have any back problem. Any other symptoms?*'

She nodded, '*You wake up every morning with swollen eyelids.*'

That did it. For the next one week I parked myself in Dr Losang Dolma Khangkar's clinic. I interviewed the Doctor, and then her patients, began a correspondence with others who had been treated, including former cancer patients, and finally wrote an article to share this experience. Dr Dolma was tall, graceful and serene, and one of the most dignified women I have ever encountered.

Her pulse reading went beyond the heartbeat. Those three fingers that she had placed on my wrists were 'listening' to twelve of my organs. Each finger takes two readings, from the right and the left side. The pressure of the fingers varies for the different organs.

Tibetan medicine is based on a combination of Ayurveda, Buddhist texts and local traditional medicinal practices. Urine analysis, for instance, is a crucial diagnostic practice and for me, a recent convert, it seemed like another miracle. I watched the doctor shaking the bottle containing a urine sample sent by a patient, examining it and announcing that the patient had had a relapse of jaundice. If anyone else had told me this story I would not have believed it. But the absentee patient was a close relative of mine who was laid up in bed suffering from relapsed jaundice. I recalled the time when I had been admitted to a hospital after a road accident and where the doctors had, for three days, insisted that I had blood sugar while my parents vehemently denied it. On the fourth day I was given a shot of insulin, which nearly killed me. Next day the hospital apologized, saying that there had been some mix-up. For three consecutive days my urine samples had been exchanged with those of a diabetic patient who had developed gangrene and was in the next room.Doubtless, while I was being given insulin shots he was being encouraged to feast on *mithai*.

Well, ever since I 'discovered' Dr Dolma and other alternative systems of medicine, I have tried to keep as far away as possible from allopathic medicine. Dr Dolma was the only daughter of an eminent Tibetan physician, Dr Tsering Wangdu Khangkar, the first girl in a family which had for many generations been doctors. Her father was determined that she had to become the 13th Khangkar lineage doctor. He personally trained and supervised her medical education. Being the only girl student in the district's medical college was not easy, but encouragement from her father and her teachers helped her to complete a rigorous ten-year medical training which included the production of medicines. As with other traditional medical practices, Tibetan doctors diagnose illnesses as well as treat patients with their own medicines. Dr Dolma became the Director of the White House Hospital in Tibet's Kyerong District — a rare distinction for a woman at the time. But this also had its drawbacks. Fearing the inevitable Chinese interference in her work, she fled Tibet with her two infant daughters. Her only possessions on that perilous journey to India were her medical books. On arrival, she had to join the other Tibetan refugees working as road-building labourers. Nobody heeded her pleas that she was a doctor and not a coolie. Then one day she reset the dislocated shoulder-bone of the road-building supervisor. The attitude of the authorities changed. What followed was a rigorous medical examination conducted by Indian Ayurveda doctors who finally allowed her to practice. Dr Dolma became the head of the Tibetan Medical Centre in Dharamsala. Later she set up her own clinic, the one I first strayed into purely by chance. Tibet's loss was our gain.

These days there is a tendency to turn to traditional healing practices only as a last resort. Many of Dr Dolma's patients were those who had been given up as hopeless cases by hospitals. As her reputation spread, so did the number of her patients. When I met her, she was seeing between 100 to 200 patients daily. Before her death in 1989 she, along with other renowned Tibetan doctors like Dr Yeshi Dhonden, the Dalai Lama's personal physician, had put Tibetan medicine firmly on the world map. Her two daughters, one in Dharamsala and the other, Dr Dolkar, in Delhi, are the 14th in the family lineage tradition of Khangkar doctors.

42

How to Steal a Billion

One would have thought that the recent announcement by China to become the biggest exporter of roses would have been greeted by flower lovers with celebration. After all, they have been cultivating roses for the last 3,000 years. Yet, their press release led to an outcry by the Western flower businesses who objected to China not paying royalty for 'internationally registered varieties of flowers'.

Perhaps they need to be reminded of some historical facts which they have conveniently overlooked. Rightfully it should be the Western flower corporates who should be paying royalties on flowers to the Chinese. Indeed, they need to pay past dues of the last 200 years. The mother or genus of what they call the modern European rose is none other than the Chinese rose which, through rather dubious means, was whisked away from its homeland and brought to Europe via Bengal (hence its two names: China Rose and the Bengal Rose). Unlike European flowers, this variety of rose flowered continuously throughout the year; hence the strong temptation to steal it from China. So, the Europeans and other businesses need to pay the Chinese for every single genetic transmutation of the rose. The amount will not be small. I believe there are over 30,000 varieties of roses today.

But why should one confine oneself only to a flower? There are other past dues owed to China that include paper, the printing press, ceramics, porcelain, glazes, the compass, tea, which was stolen; silk, which was also stolen; and, most importantly, gunpowder. The renowned Scottish scientist, Joseph Needham, Fellow of Britain's Royal Academy, wrote a seventeen-volume encyclopaedia, *Science and Civilazation in China*, tracing Chinese science and inventions. We know, therefore, that a good deal of early Western science and technology was based on Chinese knowledge. The list of inventions is so extensive that Western societies would be bankrupted settling their royalty accounts with China. Then there are other accounts to settle. They need to pay our subcontinent for their unabashed use of numerals and 'zero'. Imagine how rich we would be if royalties were due every time the 'zero' was used. Then they would have to pay royalties on cardamom, pepper and other spices, on cottons and sugarcane. The entire world would have to pay royalties to South America for maize, tomato, chilli, potato, tobacco and chocolate products. Coffee royalties would be payable to Yemen, not to speak of many other scientific discoveries of the East.

It is in the fitness of things to mention this because suddenly we are being bombarded with terms like patents, WTO and TRIP. According to the dictionary, 'a patent is a grant made by a government that confers upon the creator of an invention the sole right to make, use and sell that invention for a set period of time.' If in colonial times we were robbed of our land and resources, today we are being robbed of our diverse life forms. All the earlier inventions and discoveries over millennia by farmers are being trashed by these new regimes. Farmers are being told that setting aside seed stock for the next sowing season amounts to piracy. Instead, they are being forced to buy genetically modified seeds from multinational giants like Monsanto. Modern-day multinationals, in the name of Research and Development, are stealing from our gene banks and acquiring patents for them just as they stole the tea bush and the silkworm. One day they claim a monopoly for the name 'Basmati' and the next they want to patent Haldi. They've already pirated Neem and got patents to produce emulsions that were being produced for thousands of years by us. Next they filed cases against Indian companies, charging them with piracy for producing their own Neem emulsions as pesticides for crops and for medicinal purposes. American companies have also secured patents for the vegetable Karela — our ancient blood purifier — having based their research on traditional ayurvedic practices. These are just new mechanisms by affluent societies for stealing the wealth of knowledge of our regions. If earlier they cut off the thumbs of Bengali muslin weavers to aggressively promote English mill cloth, now we are confronted with patents on intellectual rights based on our biodiversity. Knowledge has a dollar price today because 97 per cent of all patents are owned by the developed nations.

Yet, all is not lost. Increasingly scientists around the globe are realizing the inherent dangers of these patent laws by which the farmers are getting poorer while all the wealth accumulates in the coffers of the corporate sector. Biodiversity and traditional knowledge, these scientists maintain, belong to the collective. Vandana Shiva and other environmentalists are spreading awareness amongst the farmers about the need for collective responsibility, including the creation of seed banks, as protection from the parasitic corporations. Simultaneously they are leading a crusade to change the imposed trade and patent laws and revoke patents on our biodiversity that have already been conferred.

43

Bollywood

◙

My claim to fame on my travels has not been because I am from the exotic land of snake charmers and elephants, but because I'm from the land of Raj Kapoor, Amitabh Bachchan, Rekha and Shahrukh Khan. In Egypt people ran up to me with broad smiles, but only to ask how Amitabh Bachchan is faring. In another part of the world, Uzbeks make a great effort to get past the tongue-twister of a name, Mithun Chakravarty, and then promptly ask me to convey their greetings as though I'm some close relative of his. In Kabul, taxi drivers had all the Indian stars' posters stuck on every inch of space inside their vehicles and insisted on singing the latest songs at the top of their voices. And then there was the architect from Karachi who was introduced to me in Malta. He kissed my hand, bowled me over, and then announced, 'This is the closest I can get to Rekha'. I have attended weddings in Lahore and been totally disoriented by the raucous performances of Bollywood songs and dances and indeed the bulk of my baggage to Lahore consists of the latest film magazines.

Being from the country of Bollywood has also had its disheartening moments. I walked into a music shop in Bali to buy some local music. The lady at the counter pronounced that I was from India. Full stop.

'How did you guess?'

'Your voice is just like Lata Mangeshkar's', she said, imitating the high-pitched voice.

It took me a long time to recover from that one. Later my supportive family insisted that I was actually blessed with a low husky voice.

Although I love to bask in the glory of my filmy compatriots, I am also forced to carry the weight and responsibility of the 1,000 films a year my country makes. Being lazy, I miss out on most of the super hits, and so can't answer the questions that are put to me around the world. Russians never forgave my vacant look regarding some movie, whose title, incidentally, has been changed in their language. Young Lahoris have been downright rude to me for being an ignoramus about the real things that matter, like the love life of Aishwarya. In Thailand a lady told me to convey, 'to Bollywood', that Indian films have become too violent.

Let me give one more example before we get into a post-modern analysis of the popularity of films that troubles our intellectuals so much.

An Afghan German was relating how his children love Hindi films. Germany's cinema halls have recently started showing Indian films. One day this man took his children along to watch one. When the inevitable song began, the Afghan decided to go out for a smoke. In the foyer he bumped into a German couple grumbling about the artificial film, its simplistic plot and improbable locales. He then returned to the packed hall filled primarily with Germans. The next song once again prompted our Afghan German to head out to the foyer, and there once again he met the same couple, who were grumbling even louder…

When the film ended the Afghan and his family walked out of the hall wiping their tears. He looked around and was taken aback. The Germans, including the 'protesting couple', were silently moving towards the exit. They all had red eyes, all were sniffling or wiping their eyes. They are not the only ones. Russian women have told me that they watch Indian films to have a good cry. It is cathartic, they claim.

But to return to the intellectuals and their concerns for Bollywood cinema. These so-called formulaic tear-jerkers of fantasies and illusions, of vibrant colours and strange locales, where time and space are relative and as such are a 'critique of the hegemonic euro-centric linear narratives', where prose and poetry intersperse, and pithy sayings can be uttered by both hero or villain alike, have embraced people across continents, from Guyana to Cambodia.

Whatever the cause, they have served as the best ambassadors of our country in wooing not just the gigantic diaspora, but newer audiences. Drawing upon folklore and Parsi theatre, stories and archetypes transposed onto celluloid using *Rasa* theory (depicting various emotions like love, laughter, tragedy, etc.), Indian popular cinema is the essence of India. Like a sponge, cinema soaks up anything from anywhere and everything from everywhere: locations, costumes, dances and plots. It is all there, because in our part of the world we never had rigid compartments for expression. *Lilavati*, the 12th century treatise on mathematics was, for instance, composed in verse. Prose and poetry were interspersed in many texts, fictional or non-fictional, as were realism and fantasy.

Whether it is a stroke of diplomacy or not, but the sedate French seem to have bowed to our 'make- belief 'cinema and conferred the country's highest civilian award, the Legion of Honour, to Amitabh Bachchan for his 'contribution to Indian and international cultural life'.

❈

44

Emptiness

◙

In ancient Japanese and Chinese literature we read about picnics organized just to admire the cherry blossoms and be in communion with nature, which is an integral part of life and aesthetics. It reminds me of an incident when a Japanese and a European painter were given a week to draw a duck. The Japanese just sat by the pond gazing at the ducks. The European, on the other hand, feverishly made numerous sketches every single day of the week. On the final day the Japanese, with a few bold strokes, painted the duck. This story is about the basic difference in the approach to art between two civilizations. One believes in realistic rendering, the other in the essence of things. In one part of the world individuality is supreme, in another the individual must shed his ego to be ready to learn.

I experienced this when an elderly gentleman insisted on accompanying us to the railway station where we were to catch the train. He reacted to our protests by explaining that it was his daily route to the same museum he had earlier taken us to, and that after seeing us off he would go and sit in front of one exhibit, contemplate it for an hour, and then return home.

For an outsider, sitting in front of one exhibit did seem a little far-fetched. And it wasn't as though these were enormous paintings — just fired clay jars and vases in a small Museum of Ceramics. After a month in Japan, I was beginning to somewhat grasp the Japanese mentality. My Japanese friend and I had spent two nights at the couple's house, both retired schoolteachers, in Bizen. It was a traditional house. We slept on *tatamis* on the floor. Around us were scores of elegant pots and vases presented to the couple by their students who had become famous Bizen ceramists. Bizen pottery, one of Japan's oldest ceramic traditions, is not glazed. It is left in a wood-fired kiln at a very high temperature of 1,300 degrees for some eight to twelve days. During that period, the clay, the red pine ash, and the temperature determine the subtle nuances of patterns and shades on the texture of the warm, reddish brown vessel. Each piece has the distinctive mark of a finger or the strong dash of the scalpel across it. The philosophy behind Bizen pottery is that, being handmade, it must bear visibly the imprint of the maker because of the intimate relationship between the potter and nature. This is very unlike the Chinese who, as with their cuisine, can transform a lump of clay unrecognisably into an eggshell thin translucent work of art. There are of course different schools of ceramics in Japan. Some people prefer the fine-painted glazed ceramics of Kyoto or Arita, others like the rough textured, unglazed stoneware. Pottery is such a passion in Japan that there was a time when Korean potters were kidnapped and brought to Japan.

A recent Canadian Japanese film, *Kamataki*, directed by Claude Gagnon, is about cross-cultural encounters. It has a scene where a visiting American ceramist to Japan talks down to a local ceramist Guru and lectures him about the need to shed old practices of kiln firing. The Japanese listens to him quietly and pours tea into a cup. He continues pouring into the now overflowing cup. Then he turns to the American and tells him to return home because he, like the overflowing cup, is too full of himself and therefore not ready to learn. A person desirous of learning has to be empty or without ego, the Japanese explains, and upturns the cup. The American departs, rejecting 'this Buddhist nonsense'.

The film, which incidentally also deals with unglazed Shigaraki pottery, is an example of the long path traversed since the time when Europeans were nonplussed by this approach to learning and creativity. There are many more efforts being made these days to overcome cultural barriers. What remains as a major hurdle to understanding is the concept of the impermanent nature of art in non-Western societies.

I recall my visit to Madurai. Every morning I woke at five just to go out and watch women cleaning the front entrance of their homes and drawing with rice powder, in free hand, the most intricate floral and geometric *rangoli* or *kolam* patterns on the ground. These patterns symbolize, amongst other things, a welcome to visitors. Everyday there was a new design and within minutes it would disappear — smudged and erased by the feet of passers by. Such is the impermanent nature of creativity, whose role is not to project the self. This too is the essence behind Tibetans making complex multicoloured sand paintings with vivid coloured sand to illustrate the deeper meanings of Buddha's teachings. The *mandala* takes many weeks to complete. Yet the moment the Guru's teachings are over, it is erased without a trace.

45

Two Sides of a Coin

M usa received us at the airport. His droopy face seemed even longer, emphasized by the deep furrows running down either side of his nose to his chin. Occasionally his mournful look gave way to a smile revealing gleaming gold teeth. He walked with a pronounced limp. Within minutes of our introductions Musa proudly announced that he shared his limp with that of Emir Timur. In that year, 1996, Timurlane's 660th birth anniversary was being celebrated all over Uzbekistan. An enormous bronze statue of Timurlane astride a horse had been installed in a major square in Tashkent where earlier there had been a statue of Stalin which, in turn, had replaced the statue of the Czarist General Kaufmann, the main perpetrator of ruthless colonial subjugation and rule in these parts. It was now the turn of Timur to be brought out of the mothballs of history and turned into a mascot of the newly-independent state of Uzbekistan. The traces of Timur's reign are evident in the few remaining monuments of Samarkand: the newly-restored Bibi Khanum Mosque, Shah-i Zindeh necropolis complex and Timur's own mausoleum, the Gur Emir — all great tourist attractions. Their ethereal blue domes offset by turquoise filigreed tile work contradict the image of Timur in our minds. Tourist guides explained to us how Indian craftsmen had been part of the design and construction teams. Occasionally we would throw diplomacy to the winds and tell them how 150,000 artisan prisoners from conquered territories had been made to slave on these wonderful museums under the sky, and how the very name of Timur evoked memories of unimaginable brutality in our land.

However, for his subjects Timur's reign had been a blessing. The country prospered, a vast network of irrigation channels was built, and a system of governance put in place that was the envy of visiting dignitaries, including Ruy Gonzales de Clavijo, the Spanish envoy to Timur's court in 1403. In his book, *Embassy to Tamerlane, 1403–1406*, Clavijo did not hesitate to mention Timur's barbarity, while praising Timur's numerous suburban palaces in gardens and orchards surrounding the capital city Samarkand, which, for the Spaniard, was 'so large, and so abundantly supplied, that it is wonderful'. Clavijo also mentioned an interesting detail of town planning very familiar to us all. Timur ordered a street with a covered bazaar to be built in 20 days.

> This street was commenced at one end of the city, and went through to the other. He entrusted this work to two of his Meerzas, and let them know that if they did not use all diligence to complete it, working day and night, their heads should answer for it. These Meerzas began to work, by pulling down such houses as stood in the line by which the lord desired the street to run, and as the houses came down, their masters fled with their clothes and all they had...

There is another legend surrounding Timur's tremendous impact. In 1941 a group of archaeologists arrived in Samarkand from Moscow to locate Timur's remains. An inscription on Timur's grave in the Gur Emir reads, 'We are mortal. A time will come when we will all die. If anybody encroaches and disturbs the remains of the ancestors let him suffer the worst punishment.' Ignoring the inscription and the warning given by two old men not to touch the grave for it would spell war and disaster, the archaeologists opened the grave and filmed the event. The skeleton, with one leg shorter than the other, convinced them that they had found the remains of the infamous conqueror. That was on 21st June 1941. It so happened that the next day Germany attacked the USSR.

I wonder why and how governments choose and glorify a particular historical character and ignore others. Stalin valorized some of the cruelest figures in history as outstanding statesmen, including Ivan the Terrible. In 1937 he added Timur's name to his list of esteemed military commanders. Soviet history books were immediately rewritten to depict Timur as the saviour from the Mongol-Tatar yoke. Ruling despots, it seems, seek out like-minded people in history to justify their own actions. Is that why today, Timur, a ruthless conqueror, has been valorized rather than his grandson, Ulugh Beg, the enlightened scholar monarch, famed for his work on astronomy and the observatory he built, one whose reign is associated with learning and science?

And what of the other descendants of Timur? How should we look at the Mughals of India? Apart from Aurangzeb, these emperors, especially Akbar, epitomized a high cultural point in our history.

Let us however return to droopy-look Musa's legend about himself. A few days after our arrival, when we had befriended the local Uzbeks, they told us the denouement of the Musa-Timur story. One night when Musa was in the arms of his beloved, he heard a sound outside the door. Fearing that it was his wife, Musa jumped out of the first floor window and broke his leg.

46

Rosy Prospects

⧈

Not long ago a friend of mine in Lahore asked for a catchy title for an exhibition to be held in London. She was not impressed by my suggestions so I asked an Indian Professor in Mexico to help. By the evening he had sent half a dozen options. All this activity between Pakistan, India and Mexico was over e-mail.

There is another incident I recall. I was reading a wonderful, but rather depressing, contemporary Russian novel and was getting frustrated by the unfamiliar slang. Then I hit upon the idea of e-mailing the slang to a friend in Moscow who sent me a continuous feedback.

Now imagine the Internet's use in quite another setting. The girl is on the computer and a woman arrives at her desk with a live chicken and explains how her chickens have all suddenly developed walking problems and points to the crooked legs. With difficulty, the girl and the woman get the restless chicken to stand still. A photo is taken of its legs and transmitted to a computer at another destination. The response comes in a couple of hours. The chickens have vitamin B deficiency and a remedy is provided. Later in the day, the girl looks up the e-astrology charts for some enthusiastic women or writes complaints to various government departments, or requests a birth certificate for a child that is entering school. This remarkable girl's name is Rosy of village Padinettamkudi, 35 kilometres from the nearest town in Tamil Nadu. Rosy uses her computer to make railway bookings for a man; set up the web cam and recorder for a woman's appointed time to talk to her son in the Gulf; she then contacts a city hospital to set up an appointment for a cataract operation. Come evening,

Rosy is conducting adult literacy classes for the villagers, and at weekends, English language classes for children. There is a silent revolution spreading across rural India. Rosy is just one of the many trained computer operators who earn some Rs 4,000 per month.

The computer has arrived in deep rural India.

An enterprising team of scientists and alumni from the Indian Institute of Technology, Madras initiated a programme which would provide Internet access to rural India. Known as n-Logue, this rural Internet Service provider launched its programme some years ago in Tamil Nadu. Today it covers most of south India, Gujarat, Rajasthan and Jharkand with the aim of providing Internet access to every Indian village — that means targeting over 700 million people. A bank loan of Rs 50,000 to purchase the computer and its accessories, including a printer, a web camera, a four-hour battery backup and software, was given to each kiosk operator. Villagers were trained to become kiosk operators and a software programme was developed. Some hospitals and doctors helped by providing basic training and questionnaires for the operators and they simultaneously conducted regular weekly video-conferencing with patients.

Now farmers are interacting with agricultural research institutes and veterinary institutes to find quick solutions to pests and animal ailments. For instance, a Tamilian farmer photographed a diseased *bhindi* on the web cam. This was e-mailed to the Madurai Rural Agriculture Centre, which e-mailed back the remedy. More and more farmers, by turning to *www* for market information, thus avoiding middlemen, are selling their food crops directly at auction centres, which offer better returns.

The *chanderi* weavers, once impoverished by middlemen, organized into a weavers' guild. Today they sell directly to their customers through the net and to prominent stores like Fabindia. The guild now makes profits in crores of rupees.

Bellandur village near Bangalore has become India's first e-governed village panchayat administration, covering five villages and some 10,000 people. Government data like tax collection, birth and death certificates, details of property are now available on the net. Consequently the registration of land has become simple. Bureaucratic delays, bribery and corruption have been minimized. According to Mr Jagannath, the elected president of the village and the initiator of e-governance, 'Revenue loopholes have been plugged. All government records are available at the click of a button'.

And then there is the immense opportunity opening up in education. N-Logue diversified into games, music, painting and fiction for children, and children's publishing houses like Tulika have made books available in multiple languages for the village networks. On Sundays these hubs turn into libraries and activity centres for children.

Interestingly, the majority of kiosk operators are girls or women. Drishtee is spreading e-governance, health and education in rural areas through the net. In September the Government of India announced its plan of setting up one lakh rural kiosks to serve 600,000 villages. In short, the possibilities that are opening up to villagers through the net are bringing about an exciting change which promises to turn them from areas of outward migration to places of well-being and prosperity.

✳

1. The Black Virgin in the Cathedral in Frauenchiemsee, Germany; one of over 400 Black Virgin images and shrines primarily in Catholic churches across Europe. See p. 10, 'The Black Virgin'.

2. The Black Virgin in the Theatine Church in Munich, Germany. See p. 10, 'The Black Virgin'.

3. *Josaphat Meeting a Blind Man and a Beggar.* This image dated 1469 illustrates Buddha's encounter with misery but transformed as Josaphat, the Indian prince who converted to Christianity. The story of Gautama Buddha travelled to Europe, where he was 'adopted' as a Christian Saint, who is revered to this day. See p. 13, 'Travelling Buddha'.

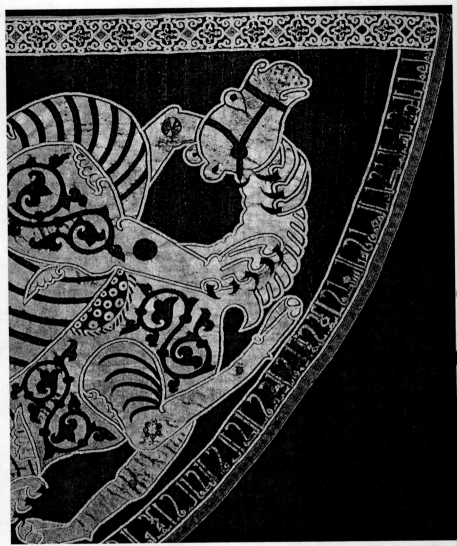

4. Detail of the Coronation Mantle of King Roger II of Sicily. It was used continuously by 48 Roman Emperors and kings from the 13th to the 18th century. See p. 28, 'Halo! Halo!'

5. The Coronation Mantle of King Roger II of Sicily decorated with Arabic script embroidered along the border. It praises the king and states that the mantle was made in the Royal workshops of Palermo in 528 (Islamic calendar). See p. 28, 'Halo! Halo!'

6. *Adoration of the Magi* (1423) by Gentile da Fabriano. Detail. Mock Arabic calligraphy decorates the long scarf and turban of the woman standing on the left. The calligraphy is also 'embossed' in the halos of the Holy family. See p. 29, 'Halo! Halo!'

7. *Adoration of the Magi* by Gentile da Fabriano. Detail. Mock Arabic calligraphy decorates the band across the man's chest. See p. 29, 'Halo! Halo!'

8. **Doorman at the Intercontinental Hotel in Phnom Penh wearing a Kaiser helmet, a short white military jacket, white gloves, a silk sarong and polished black boots over white socks. See p. 51, 'Wear with All'.**

9. Coins of Roman Emperors. Septimius Severus (193–211AD) from Libya (top), his son, Caracalla (211–217) (middle), Philippus I or Philip the Arab, a Syrian Roman Emperor who ruled from 244 to 249 AD (bottom). See p. 61, 'Blackouts'.

10. This engraved image of Durga holding a violin in one hand appeared in Gerasim Lebedev's book published in 1805. The engraving could be an altered mirror image of the Shiva image by Phillipus Baldaeus. See p. 68, 'Fiddler on the Loose'.

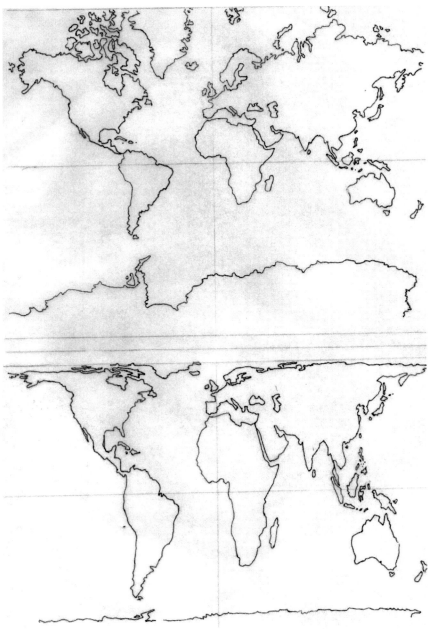

11. In Mercator's projection or map (top), the shape and size of countries north of the equator are enhanced. In Arno Peter's projection (bottom) the relative size of the countries and continents is correct, though there are distortions in the landform. See p. 106, 'Size Matters'.

12. **Bayan Tuyakbaeva, the conservationist and restorer, at the mausoleum of the Sufi Saint, Yasawi. She worked on its restoration for 30 years. See p. 114, 'Devotion'.**

椒鹽白飯魚	120
010. ไก่แช่เหล้า	
Cold Chicken in Chinese Wine.	
醉大白雞	100
011. ไก่ซีอิ๊ว	
Steamed Chinese in Soy Sauce.	
鼓汁焗雞	120
012. ลิ้นเป็ดพะโล้	
Stewed Ducks' Tongues.	
鹵水鴨舌	

13. (*From top*) Truck caption in Delhi; road sign in Delhi; shop billboard in Siem Reap; menu card in Bangkok. See p. 125, 'Linguistic Creativity'.

14. The Grave of the Armenian Sufi Saint and poet, Sarmad near the Jama Masjid, Delhi. See p. 148, 'We Owe the Armenians'.

15. Detail of the Altar Curtain from the 11th century Armenian Church of St. James, Jerusalem (*right*). The curtain was block printed in Madras in 1798, decorated with designs of South Indian plants and named in a mix of local language and Armenian. From left: *narglicar* (coconut + car or tree in Armenian, *kelucar* (banana + tree), *jakicar* (jackfruit+ tree). See p. 147, 'We Owe the Armenians'.

16. The film director, Havana Marking with Raffi, one of the finalists of the song contest *Afghan Idol*. See p. 185, 'From Havana to Kabul with Love'.

17. The author at the Wagah border, with one leg half an hour behind the other. See p. 191, 'Wagah Woes'.

47

We Owe the Armenians

□

Ashot Hindilyan graciously offered to show us around the Armenian Quarter of old Jerusalem.

'Is your name linked to India?' I asked.

'Naturally, hindi, Hindilyan. At some point of time my family traded with India. So much so I am told that I even look like an Indian. Do I?'

'Y-e-e-s, I guess so. Your nose is definitely not an Armenian nose'.

A professor at Birzeit University, Dr Hindilyan took us to every nook and corner of old Jerusalem's Armenian quarter with its narrow cobbled streets lined with stone houses, the library, the cemetery. We witnessed the ancient church service in the 11th century Armenian Church of St James. As special guests, we were shown some church treasures. These were cotton block-printed altar curtains that had been made in Madras, depicting the life of the Holy Family. A proud possession was an enormous block-printed altar curtain with images of plants. Below each image was its name in Armenian script. Hindilyan read out — *imli* — and looked up as if to ask if it made any sense.

'Of course, that's an imli *tree!'*

We tried to identify the other plants. Why anybody would make a veritable encyclopaedia of south Indian plants for an Armenian church's altar curtain is anybody's guess. Perhaps some Armenian with a passion for botany had guided the block printers while writing down the names in Armenian script for them to copy. This particular altarpiece was made in the 18th century [**Plate 15**].

The trip to the Armenian church spurred my curiosity. I remembered Mr Khachaturian, also an Armenian, who, long, long ago, had been my cousin's landlord in Bombay. So I started foraging for more information.

We are ignorant about our Armenian links that go back to the 2nd century. Armenians had once traded in many parts of India and their settlements were scattered along the coastline: Bombay, Surat, Madras, Calcutta, and later in Agra, Lucknow, Delhi, Lahore, Gwalior. Persia's Shah Abbas encouraged Armenians from Persia in the 17th century to trade with India. Their numbers swelled and soon they set up schools in Madras and Calcutta. The first Armenian language periodical was printed in Madras in 1794 and not in Armenia. It was the British who gradually forced them out, feeling threatened by their commercial expertise.

The *Ain-i-Akbari* mentions numerous Armenians who had been invited by Akbar to settle down in Agra. Mariam Zamani Begum, one of Akbar's wives, was allegedly an Armenian, as were the Chief Justice, Abdul Hai (in Armenian 'Hai' means Armenian), the Lady Doctor, Juliana, and several others.

Some claim that Sarmad, an outstanding Sufi poet of the 17th century, was an Armenian Jew, while others maintain that he was Armenian Christian. He arrived in India in 1654 from Kashan in Persia, became a *bhikshu,* and later turned to Sufism. Better known as the Naked Sufi, he attracted followers from all faiths and classes. He wrote in one of his Persian quatrains, 'I obey the Koran. I am a Hindu priest and a monk; I am a Rabbi Jew, I am an infidel and I am Muslim.' [Plate 14]

Among his disciples was Dara Shikoh, the prince-philosopher and humanist. Dara Shikoh and Sarmad were murdered by Aurangzeb. To this day people lay floral tributes on the grave of Sarmad located near Delhi's Jama Masjid.

The Zamzama canon outside the Lahore museum was made in 1761 by an Armenian gun-maker, Shah Nazar Khan, for Ahmed Shah Durrani, the Afghan invader of the Punjab. The Sikhs later captured it.

What a lot we owe the Armenians. An Armenian lady doctor opened the first nursing home in Calcutta; an Armenian conducted the first archaeological digs. There are so many unsung Armenian heroes in our history who fought the British alongside us. Colonel Jacob Petrus commanded Scindia of Gwalior's army for 70 years (1780–1850) against the British. In his extensively researched book, *Armenians in India*, Mesrovb Jacob Seth writes:

> His reputation was so high and he was so respected that the entire city of Gwalior mourned his death in 1850. Thousands including the nobility and military attended his funeral, and guns were fired ninety-five times from the ramparts of the historic Gwalior Fort, to mark his age.

Then there was the legendary Gorgin Khan, Commander-in-Chief of Mir Qasim, the Nawab of Bengal's army, and Movses Manook, a Colonel in the Nizam of Hyderabad's army. The list of Armenian military officers is long. There were historians too. Tovmas Khojamalyan wrote a history of India in 1768. It included the period of British rule, which could provide a very important source of alternative information, especially in the chapters about the infamous 'black hole' tragedy.

Was this a one-way traffic? Not at all. The 4th century Syrian historian Zenob Glak mentions that from the 2nd to the 4th century AD there existed in the Armenian area of Taron, an Indian settlement of some 15,000 Indians. It prospered for over 200 years and consisted of 20 Indian villages. They were wiped out with the coming of Christianity to Armenia. A Toran village by the name of Hindkastan existed until the early 20th century; there were other names as well — Hindukhanum, Hindubek and Hindumelik.

✳

48

A *Wondrous World Wide Web*

▣

An American lady in Lahore turned to me and commented how she admired the handsome Pakistani men of Lahore rather than the dowdy Punjabis of Delhi. This remark rather amused me because most of the men I had met in Lahore were originally from Bombay, Jullunder or Delhi, in short from our side of the border, whereas the majority of the Delhi Punjabis were formerly from places we now know as Pakistani Punjab. So who is a Pakistani and who is an Indian? My father's family spoke the Pindi Bhera Punjabi: '*aasan, jaasan*', and my mother- in- law's Punjabi has the peculiarities of Dera Ismail Khan. In our family conversations, references to Peshawar, Samarkand, Rawalpindi, Lahore and Government College are as frequent as references in conversations in Lahore to Marine Drive, Chandni Chowk and Delhi's Lodhi Gardens. We have shared histories that go back some millennia, histories that included the good, the bad and the beautiful. These shared histories of the northern region of our subcontinent would probably surprise a Keralite, who shares his history with the Yemenis, Jews, Dutch and Portuguese. He has not experienced the Partition, as did the Punjabis and Bengalis. This became apparent to me recently when a young Keralite, who had been invited to design a fashion show in Lahore, told my son, his fellow designer, that he preferred to let my son go on his own. The Keralite was reluctant to go. His past experiences had convinced him that Punjabis visiting Lahore were obsessed with eating meat and reminiscing. He explained that all they do is '*Eat meat, kababs and weep. Then they eat more meat and weep even more… I can't handle that*'.

I can understand his discomfort. For him, the boisterous and over-emotional Punjabis seem in sharp contrast to the quiet and reserved Keralites. Yet I cannot berate one culture and extol another for there is no such thing as a higher or lower culture. Each is unique. We can only talk about different cultures and ours is just one of many. It is the diversity that makes for the richness, something that was observed by Volney, an 18th century Frenchman travelling to Syria.

> When the European arrives in Syria, or in general anywhere in the East, what strikes him most in the external aspect of the inhabitants is the almost total opposition of their manners and customs to our own. …We wear short and tight clothes; they wear them long and spacious. We let our hair grow and shave our beards; they let their beards grow and shave their heads. Among us to bare the head is a mark of respect; among them a bare head is sign of folly. We salute bowing; they salute upright. We pass our life standing, they seated. They sit and eat on the ground; we raise ourselves on chairs. In sum, even in matters of language, they write in a way that is reverse of ours, and most of our masculine nouns are feminine for them.

It is because of this diversity that wisdom can be found anywhere. The Ossetians of the Caucasus have an ancient tradition. They laid down strict rules for their travellers, 'Bring back the wisdom of the country to which you have been sent, the experience of its crafts, its tales, dances and good customs.' They believed that any person returning with only negative stories about places he visited was unlikely to have left a good impression of himself in the lands he visited. Such a good-for-nothing traveller was debarred from travelling abroad for five years.

How trivial it is to talk of authenticity and roots. No culture has ever existed in complete isolation. We have within us layers upon layers of cultures, none more authentic than another, for all cultures are in the process of constant change. Cultural artefacts along with language and tales are like travelling metaphors which change their meaning as they adapt to a different culture. If Buddha can be transformed into a Christian Saint in Europe and the Arabic script can metamorphose into abstract decorative patterns for the garments and halos of saints in European paintings, so too with languages, food, clothes and ideas.

Mullah Nasr-ud-Din is a favourite character in folklore in the regions extending from Turkey to the Far East. Nobody knows if this folk hero ever existed. Regardless, there are over 14 graves of Mullah Nasr-ud-Din scattered across this region. Turkey boasts of more than one. Sharing a culture gives one a sense of inclusiveness rather than exclusion.

There is an ancient Indian concept of interdependence and interconnectedness. Indra's Web or Net is a poetic concept that was picked up by the Buddhists and recently by scientists and astrophysicists. It has even found its way into computer terminology.

The concept explains how all beings are interconnected by a fine net or web that encompasses our planet and stretches beyond into the void of the universe. At every intersection of its strands there exists a multifaceted jewel, each side of which reflects every other jewel and the entire net. And so it goes on with every reflected jewel reflecting every other without end into eternity.

49

Winter Sonata

回

History has quirky ways of knocking at our doors. How could a foreign tourist in Japan possibly make a connection between, say, Korea and red-haired youngsters in Osaka and Tokyo?

It was left to Michiko, my friend, to reveal yet another of Japan's hidden recesses: '*I'll show you the culprit behind this fashion*'.

We were headed for Japan's largest bookstore chain, Kinokuniya, in Tokyo.

'*Look*', she said.

Ahead of us loomed a gigantic hoarding covering all four floors of a building's façade. It was of a young smiling face with tousled reddish hair.

'*That is the Korean actor Bae Yong Jun, affectionately referred to as Yong Sama (Prince Yong)*.'

Michiko ignored my puzzled look as she led me into that very building, up a flight of steps, down a massive hall stacked with books, and over to one corner. Ahead of us was a long bookshelf heaving under glossies, paperbacks and posters. There he was again — smiling from ear to ear and cover to cover. A magazine was pulled out and I was told it was *Korea Today*, brought out, inexplicably, by the Japanese. Yong Sama was on every page — smiling, laughing, bowing, standing, sitting, walking; there was not a single photograph of a woman. '*What is special? Is he the latest Korean Japanese heart throb?*', I asked.

'*No-o-o!*' A loud uncharacteristically Japanese response reverberated in the silent interior, '*He is a Korean from Korea!*'

Now that was truly intriguing. On my earlier visit to Japan 25 years ago I had learnt about Japan's concerted efforts to conquer Korea; the 16th century kidnappings of Korean ceramists to Japan; the strained relations between the two countries ever since the Japanese occupation of Korea from 1910 to 1945; and the discriminatory policies towards the local Koreans.

I was not given any more details about the mysterious Yong Sama till we returned home and a DVD was immediately switched on. It was one of the episodes from a Korean soap called *Winter Sonata* with Yong Sama in the lead — the usual love story of rich boy–poor girl set in contemporary Korea. From the little I saw it seemed much more competent than our soaps — restrained acting and a visual treat of Korean landscapes. Only now did my hosts reveal the mindblowing impact of this serial in Japan. Termed variously as a Tsunami and Yongfluenza, it was aired thrice in one year. Its phenomenal success baffled sociologists, stunned the media pundits and embarrassed the government. Currently scholars and students are scouring for data in the hope of finding answers to questions that have puzzled everybody; for *Winter Sonata* succeeded where politicians and social organizations had failed.

The TV serial's most ardent fans were primarily middle-aged women who empathized with its wholesome family values, respect for elders, absence of sex and violence. Their adulation was, however, reserved for the hero who exemplified manliness and gentleness, compassion and devotion. They camped in thousands at Tokyo's airport to catch a glimpse of Yong Sama; thronged the stadium where he performed; went on package tours to Korea, visiting the film locations. In 2004, of the 5.6 million tourists to South Korea more than half were Japanese.

Not surprisingly, these ladies began to find fault with their husbands who were forced to wear rimless glasses like Yong Sama, eat Korean food, join body-building gyms, lectured on their physique and reproached for their coldness. Their usual refrain was that Korean men emote, and, unlike their Japanese counterparts, are not embarrassed to hug, laugh with abandon or even weep. They deduced that the manly physique of Korean men was due to military service. Consequently, letters were shot off to the Japanese government, demanding the reintroduction of compulsory military service to rid the Japanese men of their effeminate bodies.

There was a dramatic rise in the demand for studying the Korean language. Short-term courses proliferated across Japan with textbooks using excerpts from *Winter Sonata*. Younger women sought Korean husbands through the matrimonial columns. Our middle-aged aunties were not computer savy. Yet they wanted to read the blogs the hero wrote in the serial. En masse they enrolled for computer courses. The fact that the blogs were in Korean did not deter them. Once they had become computer literate, the women quickly mastered Google and Yahoo online translations. It was incredible! Yet this was still only the tip of the iceberg.

By far the most remarkable aspect of this entire episode was that *Winter Sonata* fans were spurred to learn more about Korean history and culture. And that is when they stumbled upon the history that the Japanese government had consistently attempted to gloss over and hide, one that was falsified and disseminated in school and university textbooks. They learnt about the atrocities committed by the Japanese colonial regime in Korea, the attempts to wipe out Korean culture in Korea and of the Koreans in Japan, many of whom had been brought back as bonded labour; they learnt for the first time the travails of the one million Korean–Japanese who were forced to adopt Japanese names and yet not provided with equal status or opportunities in Japan; people whose language and culture was projected as backward and who were being forced to assimilate in order to justify the Japanese claim that theirs was a pure, homogenous and superior Japanese culture.

A seemingly modest TV serial's social and political impact has been phenomenal. It acted as a great catalyst to bring together two nations and bridge the festering divide, opening the floodgates to adulation of everything Korean and a re-examination of history. Was this serial an exception? Would the ripples subside and the memory fade? It seems unlikely. I visited Japan three years after *Winter Sonata's* screening. The Korean boom remains. Yong Sama is acting in other serials. And his smile and hair style follow us wherever we go.

50

Linguistricks

◙

It was a strange sight. In the haze of cigarette smoke two men — one older, tall, thin and fair, the other short and dark — were slowly circumambulating the drawing room of the Delhi apartment A pair of spectacles dangled from one hand of the tall elderly gentleman. Both men seemed to be concentrating deeply on something. Neither looked at the other or spoke a word. Then suddenly the complete silence in the room was broken by loud gasps from the two dozen- odd guests as the elderly man placed the spectacles inside a lady's handbag.

This was the surprise Grigory Chukhrai had promised to show us if and when, as he put it, there was a relaxed atmosphere in our home. Chukhrai, famous for his masterpiece film, *The Ballad of a Soldier*, was in Delhi chairing the jury of the International Film Festival. I was his interpreter and within days I struck up a friendship with him and his wonderful wife, Irina Pavlovna, a bond that was to last many years. During that Film Festival our home had become the evening *addaa* of friends and young film makers, some of whose films were featuring in the Festival. It was on one such lively evening that Chukhrai decided to present his surprise by suddenly getting up from his chair and announcing that he was leaving the room. During his absence, he indicated, he wanted all of us to decide on a task for him to carry out. It would be articulated silently through the thoughts of one person who would walk beside him. So while Chukhrai was out of the room, we agreed that he had to remove the spectacles from the nose of one guest, take them round the room and place them in another guest's handbag. He returned to the room and carried out the instructions without any hesitation.

But before the stunned audience could react, one of the guests, a diehard rationalist and Marxist film maker, Saeed Mirza, leapt up and declared that he wanted to repeat the experiment. He had no intention of revealing his task to anyone and would himself walk beside Chukhrai. I translated Saeed's challenge to Chukhrai, who smiled and nodded his assent. And so it began. This time Chukhrai lifted a glass of rum and resolutely walked with it to another side-table. But there he faltered, unsure of what next to do with the glass. First he lowered the glass to the floor, then raised it above the table. After repeating this gesture several times he turned to Saeed and said in Russian, 'Concentrate'. The glass was ultimately placed on the table. Chukhrai's breathing was heavy and he seemed exhausted.

Later we asked Saeed what had gone wrong.

'Arre bhai, *the moment he lifted the glass of rum my mind went blank. I couldn't concentrate on anything. It was my fault that he fumbled.*'

What was most remarkable about these two experiments was that Chukhrai knew only Russian and both his guides had absolutely no knowledge of the language. The Russian director had 'read' their minds regardless of the language barrier. He told us that he had performed a similar feat in Cannes in a locked room with a Spaniard giving him thought directions from the adjoining room. This extraordinary ability to receive mental waves and carry out instructions of people thinking in a foreign language surpasses telepathic communication which we normally associate with one's own language. Chukhrai's ability trashes existing notions and theories about the inextricable link between language and thought, or speech and thought.

I have encountered numerous paranormal phenomena, including levitation and faith healing, but this was the first time I experienced such a challenge to conventional linguistic and psycholinguistic theories. I began a search for an explanation among linguists and scientists for this phenomenon. Their responses were identical: an ironical smile, a shrug of the shoulders and a dismissive reply. Not once did they display curiosity or interest. I persevered. In those days stray publications about PSI or parasensory investigations were trickling into the market. I read about Tofik Dadashev from Azerbaijan who had similarly displayed his ability to 'comprehend' a foreign language at the 1973 International Conference of Parapsychologists in Prague. Could it be that the form of communicated thought is unique? Messing, another famous clairvoyant, explained that transmitted thoughts became images in his mind. He did not hear but 'saw' images, which had both depth and colour.

Despite the clear evidence of such paranormal phenomena, which continue to be reported, academics, as a rule, avoid research in this field, largely for fear of being ridiculed and ostracized by their fraternity, and also because treading into this soft discipline could well shake the premise of the comfortable theoretical edifice on which linguistics rests. Science continues to rely on repetitive, measurable objective evidence, whereas many paranormal activities depend on the mental state of the person. Consequently, out-of-ordinary phenomena which cannot be duplicated in a laboratory tend to be dismissed as mysticism. Physicist Fritzof Capra, who tread the untrodden path and wrote *The Tao of Physics* was criticized by Abdus Salam.

Not surprisingly, it was the defence establishments of the erstwhile USSR and of the USA that took serious interest in the paranormal. Research and investigations funded by them were carried out in scientific institutions and hospitals. The investigations were shrouded in secrecy and had innocuous code names. The KGB and the CIA employed the services of clairvoyants, including Dadashev and Uri Geller.

A human brain has 14 billion cells, a fraction of which science has so far understood. Creative people continue to be intrigued and curious about the paranormal in our existence. Two scenes in Andrei Tarkovsky's film, *Stalker*, come to mind. In the opening scene, moments after the loud sounds of a passing train are heard, a glass of water placed on a side table in a room begins to shake. We assume that the vibrations from the train are the cause of the glass's movement. In the closing scene of the film, the Stalker's daughter, through telekinesis, wills a glass of water to move by simply gazing at it. The monochrome film format gives way to colour, and Beethoven's *Ode to Joy* from the *Ninth Symphony* underlines the Director's belief in human potential, a potential that still needs to be understood by science.

✳

51

Maali Blues

Ignorance is not bliss for me, what with being uneducated in both Latin and botany. And all because of those delicate lace-like lilac flowers which bloom every spring on the tall graceful trees that line our street. I should have just looked at them and absorbed their beauty. Instead, I suddenly wanted to possess them. Plucking one leaf from that tree was my undoing. I went from one plant nursery to another, the leaf wilting to an unrecognizable shape in my hands. Nobody could identify it. Finally, at a government nursery near Nizamuddin, the *maali* (gardener) took one look at it and casually stated, '*Mullathee*.'

'*Really. I didn't know it was a tree!*' I exclaimed.

My admiration for the tree momentarily dropped a few notches as my childhood memories of being forced to chew this *mullathee* root for a sore throat surfaced. Leaving me reminiscing, the *maali* returned with a sapling in a pot.

'*Yeh khaansee ke liye hai na?*' ('Is this a cough remedy?'), I asked.

'*Khaansee?*' The *maali* shook his head in denial. He explained that it was an ornamental tree with no connection to sore throats.

I nodded, keeping silent for fear of being exposed further. The next day I searched out my botanist colleague at the university and handed him a fresh leaf. He too gave the new leaf a bored look and muttered, 'Ah! *Milletia ovalifolia*'.

Hesitantly I ventured, '*With lilac blue flowers?*'

He nodded.

'*Not the sore throat remedy?*'

His response was a lecture littered with Latin terms. He explained that it was named after the French botanist Millet, that *ovalifolia* in Latin means egg-shaped leaves, and that it belonged to the family of Faboideae. I fled wondering why Latin had come to haunt my passion for flowers in my locality, in my city. The *maali* and my botanist colleague had a special relationship with the plants I loved and they communicated this relationship in a dead Roman language that excluded me completely. Granted that there is perhaps a need for some universal terminology, but does it have to be in a language that went into decline some 2,000 years ago, and then to have been resurrected in the 18th century and declared the purest and perfect language for defining the natural world. Latin terms, suffixes and prefixes enveloped the sciences, including anatomy and biology. The Swede, Carolus Linnaeus (1707–1778), decided to Latinise the plant world. My heart bleeds for those poor *maalis* having to learn these new names which now appear on nursery bills — *faashiya* (fuchsia), *kiran* flower (corn flower), *begum vela* (bougainvillea), *labaliya* (lobelia).

The *maali* is expected to know *Azadirachta Indica*. Why can't he just say Neem? In Persian it is *Azad Drakhata*, or 'free tree'. Perhaps what they meant was free of disease? But wouldn't it have been much simpler to just continue calling it Neem, short and bitter, rather than turn it into a Latin tongue-twister?

There is a stately, ornamental tree by the name of *Shaitan ki Jhur* (the devil's bush), a consequence of the poisonous gases it emits. It seems to be a logical environmental name as birds and animals avoid it. But the codifiers hoisted a Latin name, *Alistonia scholaris*, because its wood was used for making school slates. Now *scholaris* sounds pompous and evokes images of scholarship and learning and our landscape planners, ignorant of centuries-old local wisdom, have planted this tree along Delhi's numerous avenues. So much for environmental sensitivity.

In the real world, where Latin labels don't hang from tree branches, each plant has hundreds of names, depending on the locale. The delicate looking tree with crinkled flowers in shades of white, pink and lilac is called *jarul* in Hindi, *taman* in Marathi, *pumarathu* in Tamil, and so on. But that did not seem good enough. Native terms had to go and Latin names brought in: *Lagerstroemia reginae* — named after a Swedish merchant Magnus Lagerstroem. His claim to fame was that he received specimens of this plant and sent them on to his botanist friend, Linnaeus, who, in turn, responded and named it after his friend. It was as if since creation the plant had been just waiting to be named. But this Latinised Swedish name must have been difficult to pronounce, let alone remember, for the British. Over a period of time numerous English popular names were added such as Queen's Flower tree, Queen's Pride of India and Crepe Myrtle.

How difficult it is for all of us, and even more so for the *maalis,* who had to forget the Bhojpuri names of their childhood and re-place the entire nomenclature with two other languages, one of which only God spoke to his priests in, and the other which his colonial rulers spoke, dressed up in hats and coats.

But to be fair to the Europeans, occasionally if there happened to be a liberal botanist the original name was retained: such as Cedar or Deodar (*Deva daru*, the tree of the Gods, in Sanskrit), which in Latin is *Cedrus deodaara*. Perhaps we could say that it turned into a Sanskrit–Latin hybrid.

The passion for re-naming was endless and was not as innocent as it might have seemed. The plant kingdom was codified and organized into a system defined by European scientists on their terms, which excluded alternate approaches to nature. Plants were named after European 'visitors' to the 'New World' to signify conquest. The flower, Fuchsia, has been named after a 16th century German physician, Leonhard Fuchs; Bougainvillea derives its name from the 18th century French navigator, Louise Antoine de Bougainville, who 'discovered' this plant in South America, just as Poinsettia owes its name to Joel Poinsett, the first US Minister to Mexico, from where he brought back cuttings. I wonder if I too could re-name plants. In 1943, an Indian entomologist, M.S. Mani, named his discovery, a tiny fly,

66aa444

Prolasiopteraaeschynanthusperottetii — only 36 letters. Personally I would have preferred the fly to have been named Manius Manioptera. Fortunately there are still millions of plants without names in Latin. My family spends days searching for one such flower to call *Kalpanatham sahnium* and to build on the great possibilities of expanding Sanskrit–Latin in the 21st century.

❋

52

Stutter Nonsense

◙

The newspapers on 10th September 2008 carried a small news item captioned, 'Bilingual kids more likely to stutter, says study'. If this were true it would mean that all the children in India would take one hour to utter a coherent sentence. But why only children? Ninety-nine per cent of Indians should be stuttering. My mind went further into neighbouring Pakistan, Sri Lanka and Afghanistan — an entire subcontinent suffering from speech impediments. However, I decided to rein in my thoughts till I'd read through the news item in a corner of the International News page. It described how a team of researchers had reviewed 317 cases of stuttering children in Greater London. They had started school between the ages of 4 and 5. All the children were bilingual. But the researchers categorized them further: 69 children spoke English and a second language at home; 38 had had to learn English as it was not spoken at home; 15 of these 38 children had spoken only one non-English language before the age of 5; the remaining 23 spoke both their own language and English before that age. Thirty-one stuttered in both languages.

I, for one, honestly could not make sense of it all, including the triumphant conclusion of the researchers: 'Children who are bilingual before the age of five are more likely to stutter than non-bilingual counterparts and also find it harder to overcome this impediment according to a new study' to be 'published in the *Archives of Disease in Childhood*.'

We brought up our son to be fluent in three languages before he joined nursery at the age of three. We spoke to him in Punjabi, others spoke to him in Hindi or Hindustani. English was treated as our secret language, or so we thought, till one evening when his father remarked that it was time for his bed. Our son turned around and forcefully declared in English, '*I am not going to bed.*'

He studied in a Hindi-medium school where Sanskrit and English were also taught. In the 5th standard students had to opt for an additional Indian language. We decided that Tamil would be good. That is where we failed, as did our son. He diligently learnt all the swear words in Tamil and just about scraped through the exam, stunning the examiner enough to pass. So there he was, proficient in four languages. He has never stuttered. Every Indian is bi-or trilingual, whether literate or illiterate. With over 2,000 recognized mother tongues (a misnomer to my mind), of which 22 have been accorded official status, knowing several languages is commonplace. And so it is for all multilingual societies. Even on brief trips to other towns we instinctively pick up phrases, accents and words in the language of the area we are visiting.

Claiming with pride that one should speak only one language is a hangover of colonial times. The proud Europeans, including the French, who had proclaimed the exclusivity of their mono-lingual culture have now had to bow before the internet explosion and learn other tongues. Their earlier attempts to force reality into a straitjacket of a theory that espoused progress linked to a single-language nation state should mercifully be given a quiet burial. Yet people are stubborn. They refuse to see the need for the last rites to be performed for these outlandish theories and such news items appear at regular intervals. Debates continue about the identity problems of bilingual children. Some 'experts' maintain that knowledge of two languages inevitably lowers intelligence levels, causes confusion and even retards the children's mathematical skills. Real life does not bear this out.

I remember once showing the sites of Delhi to an American architect, Robert Venturi. In Connaught Place a beggar girl latched on to our visitor. He suddenly turned to us with an amazed look, '*How did she guess I was of Italian origin?*' She had spoken to him in Italian . Happy with the amount he gave her, she wasted no time and ran up to her next target — a Japanese. Of course it worked again; the gaping Japanese generously rewarded her for her proficiency in his mother tongue.

Many years ago a European psychologist expressed her bewilderment about Indians who seem to effortlessly switch from one language to another even within a spoken sentence. Her remarks made me conscious about something that we take for granted. Although each language has its own structures and grammatical rules, it seldom impedes shifts in our conversation. This brings us back to these rather questionable research conclusions into bilingual disabilities. Is it possible that the problems of stuttering in Greater London might have some other reasons not related to language, but rather to psychological stresses?

53

This Order, That Order

The young American architect married to an Indian had just returned from a visit to his home in New York. In the course of the evening he recalled how the moment he set foot in Delhi he felt a great sense of freedom. It contrasted hugely with his experience of New York where, on arrival, he was forced into a strait-jacket of rules and regulations while moving through corridors and standing at the end of serpentine queues, only to continue his journey on the motorway where the rules of speed determine the lane he had to drive along. His expressions were graphic — like a hailstorm of pebbles on a slate roof: oppressive, repressive, harsh and stifling. He loved all the things here which we criticize — the chaos, disorder, anarchy and mayhem on the streets, the one-man law each person follows as he skirts in and out of traffic.

The guests were nonplussed by his tirade. We are forever bemoaning our indiscipline, whether on the roads or elsewhere, and praising the efficiency and discipline of the West. And here is this young man from New York, dismissing all our notions of good and bad.

Agreed, American airports can be very tiresome with their obsession with surveillance and security checks. One has to remove one's shoes, baggage is whisked away behind a screen for a strip search, shampoo bottles are thrown into large bins. Yet we envy the West for its sense of order and work ethics. But the young architect's words kept returning to my mind and I recalled the plight of the Iranian, Mehran Karimi Nasseri, stranded at the Charles de Gaulle airport for 18 years with no European country willing to grant him refugee status. That flashback sufficed to transform my image of contemporary architecture. The steel and glass structure of Charles de Gaulle airport now seemed like a cold diabolical machine for Nasseri who had survived, not because of the French government or its bureaucracy, but through the kindness shown by the airport staff.

The most ominous airport in the world is Tel Aviv. Here, frisking, stripping, searching and interrogation have been tuned to a fine art. United Nations officials have complained that even their computer hard discs were wiped clean at the airport, others had to explain that the names in their diaries were those of their grandparents who had no connections with Palestinians. And yet this edifice of super Zionist efficiency has chinks in it. I was flying back to India after having spent some months in Palestine. Just before the plane's doors shut, armed Israeli soldiers escorted two Indians on to the plane and led them to the row behind mine. Without waiting for the guards to disembark, the men began laughing and joking in Punjabi. I turned around and asked them why they had an armed escort.

'Deported Ji. No vija'.

'You got into Israel without visas?' I was incredulous.

'Ji, we were working without vijas in Tel Aviv for the last five years.'

Maybe the Punjabis are a fine example of what the young American meant about the one-man law each person followed. They seem to skirt in and out of the most rule-bound barriers at airports. I remember queuing at Tashkent airport behind some young Afghan Sikhs with their distinctive turbans. At passport control, the woman officer asked one of them in Russian how often he had visited Uzbekistan.

'Never', he replied.

The woman leafed through his passport, looked up and accusingly declared, *'You have been here 15 times'*.

Before she could complete her sentence the man interjected in perfect Russian, *'Never in Spring madam'*.

She was so taken aback that she just waved him through.

The way officials behave at airports can be both painful and amusing. I was at Passport Control in Moscow. A young officer with an inscrutable face was sitting behind a glass partition. He transfixed me with a long, cold stare before lowering his gaze to my passport. When he repeated this a few times, I began to fidget. Perhaps there was something wrong with my passport? I began to feel like a felon. Finally, after what seemed like aeons, he handed me back my passport. Not a smile. My plane landed at Delhi airport before dawn. We stumbled out groggy with sleep, and proceeded to queue up at immigration. In front of me, across a laminated counter, sat our official. There could not have been a greater contrast between him and the Russian officer at Moscow. The Indian official was bleary-eyed like the rest of us, sipping his wake-up tea in loud slurps. Even his uniform had that saggy, sleepy look. We must have been the first lot of passengers that morning. He casually leafed through the passport and then just as casually asked me where I taught. The name Jawaharlal Nehru University was like an electric shock which instantly woke him up. His slouched shoulders straightened, his eyes opened wide. His gaze turned obsequious and with a pleading expression he turned to me, *'Can you find a suitable boy for my daughter? She's just completed B.Com'.*

It was lovely to be back home! Perhaps the American had a point. Despite everything, humaneness is what we seek.

※

54

Telling Time

For ordinary mortals, time exits in a linear sequence which has a past, a present and a future — seemingly an absolute construct which allows us to dream of a future and recollect the past. Yet even within this simple construct there is immense diversity with an endless number of permutations of the present.

First time travellers to Thailand should beware while making appointments. You might just end up missing them or waiting endlessly. Imagine sitting in a restaurant looking forward to the delicious Tom Yum Goon soup and Mee Grob noodles in the lunch menu while you wait for your new Thai friend or business colleague. And you keep sitting there gazing at the menu as the hours tick by.... It later transpires that your date understood one o'clock in the afternoon to mean seven in the evening. So remember, the Thais follow a four-part time cycle of six hours each, with the first part stretching from midnight to 6 AM, then from 7 to 12 noon, the third from 1 AM to 6 PM, etc. The time for each segment begins with the number one. Therefore, if you say that you are going to meet someone at 1, you need to be specific about the segment because 1 can be 7 in the morning, 1 in the afternoon, 7 in the evening or 1 at night. Of course there are precise terms for each segment but they happen to be in the Thai language. Just to complicate their enumeration of the present, Thais also follow the 12- and 24-hour time cycle.

Balinese time is even more complicated. Apart from the lunar and solar calendars, they have a unique Pawukon calendar of just 210 days which is neither solar, nor lunar. Then they have a three-day, five-day, and even a seven-day cycle.

Moving westwards to the Indian subcontinent in no way simplifies matters. For a start, most north Indian languages have the same word for tomorrow and yesterday, and another common word for the day-before yesterday and the day-after tomorrow, which reveals a lot about our sense of time. Furthermore, planetary conjunctions exert influences, as do the non-existent planets Rahu and Ketu, which are as crucial as the lunar and solar cycles. Then there are the multitude of New Years apart from the daily festivals linked to region, agriculture, religion, caste, sub-caste and occupation.

Do not be surprised if Tibetan parents of a newborn baby proudly announce that their offspring is a year old because they age a person from the moment of conception.

As though planetary positions and moon cycles were not enough to determine time, humans decided to further burden themselves with time-pieces. First it was the church bells signalling the passage of time, then came clocks, followed by wrist watches, and now it is the digital which enslaves us, none more so than the Japanese whose subways run to digital time: every activity has been mathematically calculated, including the time required for passengers to alight from a particular train, walk from one platform to another in order to change trains. It so happened that when some visiting Indians were told by their Japanese business associates that they would be received at the 10. 13 train at Tokyo station, they didn't take it seriously and, instead of catching the 9.47, they caught the 9.55. When they arrived at the Tokyo station, eight minutes late, their hosts had disappeared. Every second counts in Japan. This brings us to how, even in language, time has been commodified: 'time is money', 'waste time', 'employ time' 'count time', 'buy time' and 'regulate time'.

The British established Greenwich observatory to regulate global time by demarcating GMT. This served as the reference point for adding or subtracting time in their colonies, and hence tying them to England. Not to be outdone, the Russians also decided to regulate time and space. Soviet territory stretched across 11 time zones. However, all plane, train and ship schedules went according to Moscow time. Not surprisingly, I often missed my flights if

I happened to be in Samarkand or Yerevan. Mongolia has recently switched to a single time zone from its previous three, whereas China has enforced a single time zone. According to convention, when you move east you gain time. However, Pakistan, which is west of India, feels the need to be half-an-hour ahead of India.

But that is precisely what scientists have proclaimed: time is relative and may not exist at all, as in black holes. My entire perception of the night sky was transformed by my astrophysicist brother, who made me aware that I might be watching a star that no longer exists, or that I was gazing at the past when I look at Sirius, the brightest star whose light takes nine light years to reach us (a light year is the distance light can travel in a year at the speed of 300,000 km per second).

My favourite metaphor about the vastness of time is given in a Buddhist text: 'If there is a mountain measuring one yojana [a yojana can be two and a half to nine miles] and if the mountain is brushed with a silk scarf once every hundred years, then the time that is taken for the mountain to be eroded by the scarf is a *kalpa* (4,320 million years)'.

55

'Red Roses in the Snow'

❑

She sang and danced — any time, anywhere, be it in a crowded metro compartment or out in the street. Her heart-wrenching rendering of songs, about wailing guitars or galloping horses, sent shivers up the spine of listeners or forced them to inadvertently tap their feet to the sprightly dance rhythm. And language was no barrier for I have watched foreign tourists shedding tears while listening to Russian Gypsy songs. This was Rosa the Gypsy singer, dancer and actress of the solitary professional Gypsy theatre, '*Romen*', in Moscow. Her talent was spotted in a remote provincial town's bazaar where the teenage girl with large mischievous eyes and two thick plaits reaching her ankles was dancing in outsized men's gumboots. By the time we met, Rosa was already famous, yet retained her simplicity, exuberance and generosity. We hit off immediately, perhaps because I was an Indian. Soon I was discovering shared words like *raja, rani, naak* and *paani*. My memories of the evenings spent at the warm, hospitable extended family dinners were of laughter, music and the soulful duets of Rosa and her husband Petya Demetr. In those sublime moments one remembered the saying: 'A Russian dies twice; once for his country and once while listening to Gypsy songs'.

Before long Rosa, for me, came to epitomize all the numerous Gypsies integral to the 19th century Russian cultural scene. I could now distinctly visualize those graphic accounts of duels fought and abductions from Gypsy camps, tales of rivalry, jealousy and love amongst the Russian elite — all revolving around some Gypsy girl like Rosa. And then there were the poets and writers who gravitated towards the Gypsy taverns in the evenings, shedding their Europeanized lifestyles, French language and tight-fitting breeches that encased them during the day. I readily empathized with the many Russians who married Gypsies, including Leo Tolstoy's brother and uncle. Frequent references in Tolstoy's diaries reiterate his passion for Gypsy music and his recurrent escapes from the dreary high society salon parties to the uninhibited and humane atmosphere of Gypsy taverns. Inevitably, Gypsies also feature prominently in his fiction and in that of numerous other writers and poets.

I also associate Rosa with a tiny little Gypsy girl in Granada in southern Spain. Perhaps they share common ancestors: horse breeders, metal workers and musicians who embarked on their outward journeys from Punjab or Rajasthan (nobody knows for sure) in waves between the 10th and 14th centuries. They dispersed all over the world, adopting the languages and music of the countries they settled in, retaining to this day many words of their Indian vocabulary, but more importantly, their soul. In Southern Spain, Gypsy music merged with that of the Moors and the Spaniards, producing the now famous flamenco music and dance.

That tiny 6-year-old girl emerged from nowhere. Wearing outsized red stiletto heels, she confidently wobbled to the dance floor, raised her frail arms and struck a Carmen-like pose. Seconds later she began dancing in the silence of a dark Gypsy tavern where two of us were the sole customers sipping coffee. A guitarist, most likely her father, watched the child with a smile, then gently plucked at his guitar strings. Three Gypsy ladies, sitting huddled up in one corner, began clapping rhythmically to the red stiletto beats. The dance and the song that followed miraculously awakened the tavern's slumbering energy. The plaintive dirge of the woman singer brought a lump in my throat. I recalled Garcia Lorca's poem: 'Oh Gypsy pain/ Pain so clean, and, always so alone/ Oh pain from hidden streams/ And the distant dark of dawn.'

It was the year 1971 and we were in General Franco's Granada, in a country where the 500-year-old ban on the Gypsy language remained in force; a military regime that had forbidden the works of Lorca, Spain's greatest 20th century poet, who grieved over the tragic fate of Moors and Gypsies at the hands of the state. Terming the Gypsy songs as 'the scream of dead generations, a poignant elegy for lost centuries', Lorca exposed Spain's hidden reality and, by implication, that of Europe where, since their arrival, the Gypsies were persecuted, ghettoized, terrorized, sterilized, forcibly settled, their language and culture forbidden. Simultaneously they were vilified as thieves and vagabonds. Their hardships culminated in the extermination of between 500,000 to 800,000 Gypsies in Hitler's gas chambers (but unlike the Jews, their cause was never taken up). I wondered how many Rosas were amongst the murdered and how many Rosas suffered in the 1950s and 60s in the face of the forced settlement programme in the USSR.

Yet, the only crime of the Gypsies was that they did not subscribe to the values and belief systems of the European states. The Gypsies' innate love of freedom included a nomadic lifestyle and disregard for geographical boundaries, disdain for material comforts, yet pride in, and the determination to uphold their own customs and laws. Consequently, European governments did all in their power to force them into submission.

The irony is that even as the governments pursued the Gypsies, leading European writers (Cervantes, Hugo Victor, Prosper Merime and Pushkin) glorified their tenacity, their indominatable will to survive and their freedom-loving nature, turning them into symbols of liberty versus state tyranny.

In time, democracies replaced Fascist governments, yet even today the social stigma remains. The Gypsies are being issued identity cards in Italy, denied work in Slovenia, and continue to be ostracized and hounded everywhere. A substantial percentage of Spain's youth want them expelled from the country; a country which, even after 500 years of their residence in Spain, till recently enlisted the Gypsies as migrants. Meanwhile the Spanish government's tourism brochures lure tourists with promises of the famed Gypsy flamenco dances.

Rosa died in 1985. She was only 42. There is a refrain from one of her songs: 'Oh! Don't wake me up/Till the sun rises for the Gypsies'...

Since Rosa's death numerous world-wide organisations of Gypsies have sprung up, challenging ingrained perceptions and tackling problems pertaining to their lives, while simultaneously forging links with fellow musicians worldwide — determined that '*the sun will rise for all the Gypsies*'.

Rung Interpretation

◉

Not so long ago, Bhajju Shyam, an Indian folk painter, went to London where he had been commissioned to decorate an Indian restaurant. It was an unforgettable experience for him and on his return he made paintings of his impressions of that city. One painting depicted the morning rush hour: ant-like humans in black clothes emerging from the dark caverns of the earth (metro stations) and scattering in all directions.

Although taken for granted, colours are an integral part of a cultural ethos. All our clothes and festivals are a riot of colour. We celebrate Holi, a festival of colour, the harbinger of summer. Vibrant colours are part of the Latin American, Chinese, African and Asian ethos. We have no hesitation in mixing and matching colours, which might shock European sensibilities and principles of colour matching. Each culture's sense of colour is coloured by its surroundings and by the availability of dyeing agents, which include a wide spectrum of plants, minerals and insects. The mauve and purple colours of the traditional skirts of Mexicans and Costa Ricans were traditionally derived from the pigment of the caracola marine snail's mucus which reacts to the sun's rays by turning from milky white to green and finally purple.

Colour travels brought about changes in dress, painting and aesthetics. The red dye from the cochineal insect was exported from Central America to China, whereas the red from the kermes insect travelled across Persia, Afghanistan and Central Asia and was used for the numerous shades of rich, red hues in the carpets. The travels of indigo and the Bengal riots against the British whose insatiable appetite for the dye forced a mono-crop cultivation in the region, are well known. Ultramarine (a shade of blue derived from lapis lazuli), reached Europe in the 13th century and is a derivative of the Italian word, *oltramarino*, or 'another sea', although its source was the mountainous terrain of Afghanistan. The famous blue-and-white Chinese porcelain is made of cobalt glaze. Cobalt oxide, with a long history of bright blue glazed tiles in Persia, was exported to China.

The Phoenicians, whose name is derived from the Greek word *'phoenis'* or 'the purple people', had settled along the Lebanese coast. They were dyers and traders of a highly sought after purple dye derived from the mucus of murex, a marine snail. Tyrian blue similarly gets its name from the town of Tyre where the Phoenicians manufactured the dye. There was a time when purple, ultramarine and deep red were so rare and expensive in Europe that their use in clothing became the monopoly of the church and royalty.

In every culture, colours are given a complex symbolism. Amongst the Comanche of Central America, the word *'ekapi'* signifies 'colour', 'circle' and 'red'. In the past there was one word for 'red' and 'beautiful' in Russian, and hence the word, 'Red Square'. In Punjabi, *'laal'* is both a form of endearment and signifies the colour red. Vivid red at the entrances of Chinese shops, homes and temples symbolizes good energy. This notion is shared in parts of India where red is the colour of the bride's dress. Conversely, red, in the west, was associated with the sacred blood of Jesus, and thus was taboo in dress and painting. It was also associated with sin, guilt (e.g. catch red-handed) and prostitution.

The depiction of the Indian goddess Kali, the creator, preserver and simultaneously the destroyer of evil, is black. In Europe, black, on the contrary, is the colour of death and mourning, and is associated with evil. The synonyms for black are gloomy, threatening, diabolical, and hence: black magic, black thoughts, black deeds. Curiously though, black is also the colour of the habit of nuns and monks. During Elizabethan times in England there were laws defining dress and colour codes for the various strata of society. Jet black, an expensive dye to make, was assigned to the aristocracy. Over time black suits and dresses came to signify authority, prestige and elegance.

For translators, colours can prove a veritable nightmare of cultural transference. Take the ancient Indian tale of Nala and Damayanti. When Nala, the king, loses his kingdom in gambling and is forced to retire to the forest, his wife, Damayanti, changes into *gerua* (earthy brown) coloured clothes, signifying asceticism. In one Russian translation of the work, the *gerua* colour is rendered as black, a symbol of widowhood in Russia. Thus, the absence in Russian of both an equivalent colour and symbolism has resulted in an alien cultural entity entering the translated text.

Royall Tyler, the translator of the famous eleventh century Japanese novel, *Genji Monogotari*, acknowledges defeat and apologizes for his inability to translate the numerous Japanese colour terms into English due to lack of equivalents. A random check in the novel's Glossary of Terms reveals that there are over 20 Japanese terms for the varying shades of blue. How then could an anthropologist like Alan Macfarlane claim that 70 per cent of the Chinese and Japanese were myopic due to their script, and therefore could only distinguish five colours: black, white, light red, dark red and ultra-marine; or that most Asians are unable to distinguish between blue and green. His fellow anthropologist, Victor Turner, went even further in his outrageously racist assertion that the African notion of colour was confined to biological functions and there-fore their predominant colours were red, white and brown. It is therefore hardly surprising that such 'theories', presented with a veneer of objectivity and scientific rationale, produced stereo-types in European minds.

Yet people have matured and can take such 'scientific truths' with humour. Eventually, our Asian sensibilities remain emotionally linked to colour, whereas in the West, where reason and logic prevail, Newton and Goethe's interpretations of colour are very seriously regarded. Witness the new breed of professionals in advertising known as the colour-trend managers. The chairman of an international ad agency, WCRS, states, 'Colour is all about signalling, and behind that lies sex'!

✳

57

African Indians

◙

There is a well-known story of a woman who lost her keys in her house but was searching for them under the light of the street lamp. She explained to a passerby that her house was in darkness so she had decided to search for them where there was light.

Like that woman, I had been searching for our links with diverse countries, but had ignored the most obvious — our neighbouring continent. In those days I was clueless about the 250,000 or more African Indians living across India. Yet the recurring earthquakes in our northern regions, signs of the subcontinent's continuing thrust northwards, should have alerted me. There are marine fossils in the upper Himalayas, river pebbles in the Kangra hills, seashores and riverbeds of an Africa millions of years ago from which our subcontinent had drifted away. How was it that the Onge, Jarawa and Sentinelese African tribes had been residing in the Andaman and Nicobar islands for over 20,000 years?

The moment my thoughts turned to Africa, a veritable mine of information was revealed. I found that scientists and historians had discovered not only our DNA links with Africans, but also ancient trade contacts, including those with Ethiopia when a large horde of 4th century AD gold coins was found in Mangalore. They had been issued by King Ousanas and his successor Ezana of the Aksum kingdom (Ethiopia) which had flourished between the 1st and 7th century AD. India, it transpires, was inundated with merchants, sufi saints, sailors, soldiers, doctors, musicians, army generals, poets, ministers and kings from the Sub-Sahara who had even ruled parts of India up to 1948. Their traces remain in documents, coins, numerous monuments and entire cities which they built. More importantly, their African Indian descendents still live primarily in the Deccan. A recent book, *African Elites in India*, richly illustrated with photographs and miniature paintings, focuses on the 15th–20th centuries. It explores the contribution of the African elite to Indian state polity and culture, emphasizing that the book aims 'to stimulate readers to rethink preconceptions'.

Take Aurangabad, a city I've always associated with Aurangzeb and his tomb and a getaway to the Ajanta and Ellora caves. Now I discover that not far from Ellora lies the tomb of a certain Malik Ambar, the real founder of Aurangabad. This gentleman was an Ethiopian from the village of Harar. Ambar arrived in India around 1570 and began to serve another African, Chingiz Khan, the Peshwa of the Ahmednagar Kingdom. This was a breakaway of the Bahamani kingdom, which had in its army soldiers from diverse African regions. Malik Ambar rapidly rose to important state positions and became the de facto ruler of the kingdom of Ahmadnagar for 26 years till his death. For two decades every attempt by the Mughal armies to conquer the South was thwarted by the guerrilla tactics of Ambar's forces. Malik Ambar became Jehangir's nightmare. The Mughal Emperor even commissioned a painting depicting the severed head of Malik Ambar with an arrow through his mouth, impaled on a long pole. In the centre of the painting and facing Ambar's head is Jehangir in regal splendour, a raised bow in hand, standing atop the globe. These were the Mughal Emperor's fantasies, because his arch enemy and adversary died a natural death in 1626, one year before Jehangir's demise. Had Ambar lived on, historians suggest, the fate of the Deccan might have been different.

Having spent his lifetime in battles, it was natural for Malik Ambar to concentrate on the construction of numerous forts including Khandar, the Ambarkot in Daulatabad and refortify Ankhur . He founded a town near Khidki village with a vast network of underground water canals; a church, a Chita Khana for scholars from all over the country, the Ambar Palace, numerous mosques including the Juma Masjid, and his own tomb outside the city. Much of this architecture remains. After his death, his son renamed the town Fatehnagar and subsequently, when Aurangzeb was sent there as Governor, the town became Aurangabad.

In the Bijapur Sultanate, Malik Sandal, the Ethiopian, was responsible for the construction of numerous buildings whose magnificence was comparable to the Mughal architecture of the time. Other marvels of architecture constructed by Ethiopians are scattered across the Deccan and Gujarat, including the Siddi Said Mosque in Ahmedabad.

Ethiopians or Habshis (from the Arabic of Abyssinian) were also known as Siddis and held governorships and ministerial posts. In the reign of Razia Sultan (1236–40) her main advisor and minister was an Ethiopian. Aurangzeb handed over charge of the Mughal navy to Sidi Sumbal. Habash Khan served the Mughals and became the Kotwal of Delhi. Atish Habshi was the Governor of Bihar and later Deccan in the mid-17th century and the hereditary physicians of the Nawabs of Junagarh were Africans.

Janjira is located 40 miles from Bombay along the Konkan coast. It was the capital of a kingdom ruled by the Ethiopians from 1618 till 1948 when they ceded to the Indian state. In 1791, a member of the Janjira family established the state of Sachin in Gujarat. An Ethiopian dynasty briefly ruled Bengal from 1487 to 1493. The terms Habshi and Siddi could well be generic terms for the migrants from diverse African regions, which we now know as Nigeria, Sudan, Mozambique and Ethiopia, who adopted India as their homeland. None of this should come as a surprise. Europe had Popes and Roman Emperors from Africa, and similarly Africans, by their presence in India, enriched our cultures. One eagerly awaits more information from researchers engaged in the written and oral traditions, customs and music of African Indians, the rhythms and melodies of Goma dances, and the different types of drums whose beats echo in some far away African region.

❋

58

From Havana to Kabul with Love

◻

They had discreetly placed the DVD on our side table, as befits the well-mannered English, and then departed for Kodaikanal. It was their daughter's latest documentary. During their stay with us the previous year, they had tried to hide their anxiety about their daughter's choice of location and subject for such a movie at such a time.

'*But Stacey*', I told the mother, '*didn't you cover Bolivia and other war-torn Latin American countries for the* Guardian? *How can you expect Havana to be different? She's taken after you. She will never opt for some ordinary subject. Remember the last film she made was about some young handicapped men who were intent on doing a striptease on stage?*'

Only Havana could have come up with that idea. Mind you, we had all liked that film when we saw it. Over the years we had grown accustomed to Havana's surprise knock on the door, a haversack on her back; Havana disappearing across the sand dunes of Rajasthan only to re-emerge a month later, bejeweled with nose and ear-rings, pierced eyebrows (this came to an abrupt end when she was stripped at Heathrow airport and searched for drugs). She was completely at home in India, having first come here as a 2-year-old with blue eyes and a mass of red curls framing her round freckled face. Naturally she was a favourite with everybody on Delhi streets. Nobody could ignore her presence. Last year Havana had flown to Delhi from Kabul for just a day, leaving behind energy and a bag full of dried *shahtoot* fruit. And now her debut feature documentary film was beckoning us.

We watched the film for over an hour on a laptop screen. As the last titles of the film scrolled on the screen, we knew this film was a winner. Just a week earlier it had been accepted for the 2009 Sundance Film Festival in the US. This is a 'must see' film, refreshingly free of didactics and sermons, a film whose focus is on an Afghanistan that world media has ignored. Only a person with boundless human compassion could have made such a film. Havana had once again seamlessly entered Afghan society and won each person's heart. That is the only explanation for the total abandon of every Afghan child or an aspiring singing star on camera. They have opened up their souls to this blue-eyed, red-haired foreigner.

Afghan Star is about the immensely popular television reality show of that name. The documentary narrates the final episodes of the singing competition for which over 2,000 participants from across the country, including three girls, had competed. A third of the country participated in it and SMS'd their votes on their mobiles. The camera follows the four finalists and captures a kaleidoscope of preparations for the show funded on a shoestring budget; the excitement of the viewers huddled around a TV set in a tiny home, then in a shop; little boys selling batteries on a cart (in the event of a power cut during the show), a woman constructing a makeshift TV dish on her roof; a family excitedly discussing their favourite singer [**Plate 16**].

The *Afghan Star* is a celebration of life, of hope and determination. After 10 years of Taliban ban on music and TV, the Afghans, with an ancient musical tradition, are waking up from their enforced slumber. Daoud Siddiqui, the host and creator of the show and the real star, explains, '*There are many ways to persuade people to get together*'. He chose to unite people from across the country by hosting the *Afghan Star* singing competition. Daoud and the contestants believe that songs can make people turn away from guns.

Filmed images of the empty shell of a bombed cinema hall, of abandoned tanks and gun-toting policemen are reminders of the constant dangers and a precarious existence. Yet the four finalists from different parts of the country are undeterred by these sanctions and threats. Some of the most moving scenes show the two girl contestants, one of whom had secretly taken singing lessons under the very nose of the Taliban moral police. The other girl, equally passionate about music, dreams about becoming a singing star one day. In her final performance she not only sings but dances on the stage, fully aware of the repercussions. Death threats follow and she has to go into hiding. But she remains defiant, unrepentant and courageous, certain that one day she will change people's mindsets. The camera follows her to her hometown and shows poignant scenes of a family reunion. An old film clip from the 1980s is inserted, which shows girl students with short hair and short dresses on Kabul university campus; a concert with the university rock band accompanying a girl singer in trousers on the stage. Threats by the Taliban and the religious heads were only one of many impediments Daoud Siddique and the contestants of *Afghan Star* had to face. There were three bomb explosions in Kabul within the first week of Havana's arrival. But the zeal and determination of the young Afghans was so infectious that she took the plunge, braving journeys into dangerous terrain, living in sub-zero temperatures and constant power cuts during her three months in a country still at war.

Our predictions about the film came true. Havana's *Afghan Star* did indeed receive the World Cinema Award for Best Director as well as the Audience Award at the Sundance Film Festival. The media hype around *Slumdog Millionare* had overlooked this extraordinary and inspiring film, ironically, also about a reality show but based on fact, not fiction. *Afghan Star*, both as a reality show and as a film, reiterates faith in the human being and proves the existence of alternate paths to reach out and engage with people instead of looking down at them as patients in need of help.

❋

59

Phantom Foes

▣

*D*on Quixote appeared at my bedside two years after the world had celebrated the 400th anniversary of the publication of its first part in 1605. I decided to re-read this satirical novel. It is not that I take a perverse pleasure in reading about an old man who has been ridiculed, beaten and scoffed at for most of the 1,000 pages of the novel, a fate he suffers because he is the chivalrous, quixotic, idealistic, impractical Knight with the Sorrowful Face who charges at windmills because he is determined to do good in an age when chivalry was dead. No, my decision to re-read this voluminous masterpiece was motivated solely by new information about the 800 years of Moorish and African presence in Spain that had begun to appear after being kept under wraps for centuries. The second part of *Don Quixote* (published in 1615) was being written during the implementation of the 1609 Edict which forcefully expelled the remaining Moorish population from Spain.

I wanted to discover meanings beyond the obvious references to Moors, including Cervantes' use of the ambiguity device suggesting that the real author of the novel is a Moor; Spanish word derivatives from Arabic; the return to Spain of an expelled Moor in disguise and others. Some critics claim that the five years of captivity in Algeria made Cervantes unsympathetic towards the Moors (or Moriscos), and that explains the paucity of references to Spain's Moorish connections.

Such justifications are no longer satisfactory because Cervantes lived in the most repressive period of Spanish history. It was a time of expulsion of the Moors; of forcible religious conversions; strict state and church censorship; and importantly, of the Inquisition, when people, books and libraries were being consigned to flames. Cervantes was 19 years old when the 1566 oppressive decree was issued banning Moorish dress, food, language, customs and even warm baths. That decree had led to riots across the country and it took the government two years to quell them. After that the Morisco population was deported from Granada and its property confiscated. But the Moors were an industrious community and the mainstay of Spain's economy and agriculture. Their expulsion resulted in an economic collapse. It did not seem plausible that writer could have remained immune to the extensive trauma and misery of his countrymen.

I came to the famous chapter on Quixote's battle with the windmills and researched the origins of windmills in Spain. The windmills were set up in Spain by the Moors in the 12th century. The earliest mention of them can be found in 7th century Persia and Afghanistan. Now if you substitute the term 'windmills' with 'Moors' (or Moriscos), the meaning of the text undergoes a dramatic transformation — so completely at variance with our conditioning. Heroic Quixote, on seeing 30 or 40 windmills, turns to his companion, Sancho Panza, and says, '...thirty or more enormous giants with whom I intend to do battle and whose lives I intend to take and with the spoils we shall grow rich, for this is righteous warfare, and it is great service to God to remove so evil a breed from the face of the earth.'

This is the hidden context within the text. It is not a dreamer who is fighting the phantom windmill enemies. It is the Spanish Crown, with its delusions of grandeur, that is fighting a chimera, tilting at windmills by indulging in violence and injustice against the very people who introduced the most significant innovations in hydraulic engineering, horticulture, agriculture and wind energy, and contributed to turning the country into the most advanced and prosperous European state. Later in the book, Quixote observes: 'The greatest achievement is to lose one's reason for no reason', clearly a reference to the Spanish government of Cervantes' time.

The windmills are only one of the numerous Moorish engineering feats portrayed as 'enemies' in Don Quixote's imagination. He 'attacks' an enemy's castle, in reality a watermill used for grinding wheat; in another scene he is stopped from engaging in battle with six huge fulling mill hammers on water wheels, and which were interchangeably thumping several pieces of woollen cloth to thicken it.

Another skirmish takes place when Don Quixote mistakes two approaching clouds of dust raised by migratory flocks of sheep for two military forces. Undoubtedly these were the famous Merino sheep whose wool, termed the golden fleece, was Spain's most valuable export commodity. Merino sheep were introduced in Spain in the 12th or 13th century from Morocco or Tunisia by the Beni Merin (hence 'merino') Dynasty of North Africa. Sheep rearing, spinning and weaving centres promoted by the Moors soon turned wool into a thriving and lucrative business. When the last Moorish ruler was expelled from Granada in 1492, Merino sheep and export of its prized wool became the property of the Spanish Crown. Up to the 18th century, it was forbidden, on pain of death, to export the sheep or merino wool. In Cervantes' lifetime, inhuman government policies had led to the decline of Merino sheep. The estimated stock of 3.5 million sheep in the 1520s was reduced by a fifth by 1564 due to the expulsions of and terror tactics towards the Moors who, though no longer sheep-owners, were retained as the labour force tending the sheep. This battle with the sheep can be re-interpreted as yet another chimera being fought by the crown.

Cervantes through allusions, ambivalence, oblique hints, Aesopean means and cryptic remarks, emerges as a great humanist with an innate empathy for the persecuted Moors, not shying away from any topic concerning Spain's 'iron age'. According to him,

> ...historians must and ought to be exact, truthful, and absolutely free of passions, for neither interest, fear, rancour, nor affection should make them deviate from the path of the truth, whose mother is history, the rival of time, repository of great deeds, witness to the past, example and adviser to the present, and forewarning to the future.

❋

Wagah Woes!

◻

Her smile is bewitching. A bank clerk has only to look up and that habitual 'No' freezes on his lips as he beholds her radiant smile. And when she gently says 'Mera passbook bhar deejiye' (Please update my passbook'), his jaw drops. It's the same story wherever she goes. In government offices the baboos instantly cease their gossip, stop sipping their tea and ignore their clients to sort out her problems; the subziwalla (vegetable vendor) lowers his prices for her and the bus conductor makes sure she gets a seat. That is Valerie, a 5ft 11-tall salwaar kameez clad lady from the US. She is one of a few foreigners who speaks the local language in the Kangra Valley in Himachal.

Valerie has made Sidhbari in Kangra her home for over a decade and this story is about one of her experiences. Every six months, foreigners with long-term visas have to leave the country, get their passports stamped, and return. This, I am told, is a reciprocal gesture of the Indian government to USA laws for Indians in America. The foreigners residing in the Kangra Valley usually head for Nepal while others head for more distant lands.

We were sitting together discussing this impending biannual ritual. Valerie was dreading the long haul to Kathmandu on her own. It suddenly occurred to me that the Wagah border could provide an alternative and shorter route out. I had been there once and had watched enviously the ease with which Europeans and Americans just ambled across the border. It was a privilege denied to the Pakistanis and the Indians. We had to derive our satisfaction by sitting in the mini amphitheatre that had been constructed for our entertainment as it serves as a vantage point from where one can watch the border guards of both sides stiffly goose-step, marching up and down on either side of the white line drawn across the road that connects the two countries. What an incongruous sight that is, so reminiscent of the Nazi soldiers. The border guards march by first lifting their legs up to impossible heights, almost up to their chins, and then bringing them down with a bang. The Pakistani guards replicate the same goose-step. I couldn't tell whether it was the height of the raised legs or the banging down that was meant to emphasize their respective patriotic zeal. Were they trying to outdo each other through this ludicrous march? They seemed more like mechanized toy soldiers. At the flag-lowering ceremony every evening their body language, I was told, becomes even more aggressive.

I had gone to Wagah for a Peace Meeting where my father was the Chief Guest. On the dais, a loudspeaker was positioned to face Pakistan. During the meeting, one speaker after another extolled the virtues of peace and friendship with the people on the Pakistan side of the border. I asked one of the organizers whether their speeches could be heard in Pakistan. He assured me that there was no question of the sound reaching Lahore. An aged Punjabi gentleman got up and recounted how, in the old days, he used to cycle to work daily from Lahore to Amritsar. It took him nearly two hours. I wondered how he would have judged that time now, for governments have strange ways of promoting national identities and one of them is to put the clock forward or back. We walked up to the white line that divided our countries. We pleaded with the Pakistani guards to allow us to step onto the other side of that white line. We were permitted to do so with one foot only as it was strictly against regulations to be let in without a visa. I placed a foot in Pakistan. My one leg was half an hour behind the other one [**Plate 17**].

Returning to the present, I emphatically announced that Wagah was the best option for Valerie. It was close by, a mere five-hour bus journey to Amritsar, and another 30 kilometres from there to Wagah.

'*Stay for a few days in Lahore, which you will love, and return*'.

We caught up with each other a few months later.

'*Did you like Pakistan?*' was my first question.

'*I never got there. Just walked across the border and walked right back.*'

'*Why?* I wailed.

'*It seemed so desolate on the other side of the border. Hardly any vehicles or people.*'

'*If only you had spoken a bit of Hindustani they would have eaten out of your hands.*'

'*I did.*'

'*Then?*' I wouldn't let go.

'*The Pakistani border officials were dumbstruck.*' '*Aap itni achchee Urdu bolte hain*' ('*You speak such good Urdu*'), *they said. I kept insisting that I spoke Hindi, but they just nodded, and repeated with a smile,* 'Kya baat hai, bahut khubsoorat Urdu bolte hain…' ('How amazing. You speak such beautiful Urdu'). *Each one of them invited me to visit his home. They offered me tea and mithai and were so kind. And just like in India, I was bombarded with endless questions about my family, children, work. The moment they discovered that I was a physiotherapist one of them yelled out to somebody outside. Immediately the tiny room filled up with all the marching giants. One man pointed to his knees and asked me if I could help him. He was in agony. That hard stomping of feet had affected his knees. Another took off his socks to reveal his swollen heels and ankles. They were a terrible sight — those poor guards. I demonstrated a few exercises that could help them. At that moment I regretted not carrying my Physiotherapy Manual of exercises …. To cut a long story short, that lecture demonstration seemed to have gone on for quite a while. All of a sudden I realized that the sun had set and I chickened out. I couldn't bring myself to visit Lahore alone, without Jimmy. Even the Pakistani officials could not understand my decision to return.*'

This time Valerie (along with her husband, Jimmy) is once again heading for Wagah. Her baggage includes several xeroxed manuals on leg and foot exercises which she plans to distribute to the guards on both sides of the border before enjoying a ten-day holiday in Pakistan.

✳

About the Author

A well-known academic, Kalpana Sahni is a scholar of remarkable diversity. Her extensive writings on Russian literature and culture as well as her Central Asian fieldwork in the old *mohallas* of Samarkand, Bokhara, Turkestan and Dushanbe have given her a unique sensibility about interconnected cultures. She has been consulted by The Aga Khan Foundation and the Rolex Mentor and Protégé Arts Initiative Programme. Sahni spent her early schooling years in Moscow where she returned to do her doctorate, after which she joined the faculty of the Jawaharlal Nehru University in Delhi. Professor Sahni's publications include two books, *A Mind in Ferment: Mikhail Bulgakov's Prose* and *Crucifying the Orient: Russian Orientalism and the Colonization of Caucasus and Central Asia*, and three edited books on literature.

01341 1660077 3

DATE DUE	RETURNED

CPSIA information can be obtained
at www.ICGtesting.com
Printed in the USA
FFOW01n1311140916
27671FF

9 781138 662650